MILLI$NAIRE™ SECRETS

Millionaire Selling Secrets: How to Become a Millionaire Now By Using These Ten Simple, Fast, Easy, Proven Secrets of Persuasion!

T0166086

MILLIONAIRE SELLING SECRETS

How to Become a Millionaire Now Using These Ten Fast, Easy, Proven Secrets of Persuasion!

Brett Bacon

iUniverse, Inc.
New York   Bloomington

Millionaire Selling Secrets
How to Become a Millionaire Now Using These Ten
Fast, Easy, Proven Secrets of Persuasion!

MILLIONAIRE
SECRETS is a trademark of Contract Vantage Advisory Group Corporation. Millionaire Secrets™ is a new series of books, ebooks, audio books, CDs, courses, and eNewsletters on success and business topics, with offices at 101 Shattuck Way, Suite 4, Newington, NH 03801. Web site: *www.brettbacon.com.* Telephone: 603-431-1220. E-mail: *info@brettbacon.com.*

iUniverse books may be ordered through booksellers or by contacting:

iUniverse
1663 Liberty Drive
Bloomington, IN 47403
www.iuniverse.com
1-800-Authors (1-800-288-4677)

ISBN: 978-1-4401-5976-3 (sc)
ISBN: 978-1-4401-5977-0 (dj)
ISBN: 978-1-4401-5978-7 (ebk)

Printed in the United States of America

iUniverse rev. date: 8/10/2009

Brett Bacon is coauthor of the book:

Wake Up ... Live the Life You Love: In Service, Copyright 2009.

From the Best-Selling Series

Wake Up ... Live the Life You Love

Is service something that we do only for others? Perhaps we should serve only our own needs and desires in order to get what we want out of life. These are the dilemmas we create when we consider what we should live for.

It is through service to others that we find true fulfillment. We avoid serving our selfish interests and, at the same time, escape slaving away on some path that is not truly what we desire to do.

In this book, you will find uplifting stories of individuals who did just that—found their own passion and aided others in the process. You can join them. Let these inspirational authors show you how to serve yourself best by serving others.

Coauthors include: Steven E, Lee Beard, Brian Tracy, Dr. Wayne W. Dyer, and Ruben Gonzalez.

You can order this book, *autographed by coauthor Brett Bacon*, for a limited time only at www.brettbacon.com.

This book is available at quantity discounts for bulk purchases. For more information, please call 1-866-480-1220 or go to *www.brettbacon.com*.

Disclaimer

The author and publisher of this book and the accompanying materials have used their best efforts in preparing this book. The author and publisher make no representation or warranties with respect to the accuracy, applicability, fitness, or completeness of the contents of this book. The information contained in this book is strictly for educational purposes. Therefore, if you wish to apply ideas contained in this book, you are taking full responsibility for your actions.

The author and publisher disclaim any warranties (express or implied), merchantability, or fitness for any particular purpose. The author and publisher shall in no event be held liable to any party for any direct, indirect, punitive, special, incidental, or other consequential damages arising directly or indirectly from any use of this material, which is provided "as is," and without warranties.

It is sold with the understanding that the author and publisher are not engaged in rendering legal, accounting, or other professional advice. As always, the advice of a competent legal, tax, accounting, or other professional should be sought.

The author and publisher do not warrant the performance, effectiveness or applicability of any books or Web sites listed in this book. All other books, informational products, and Web sites referenced in this book are for information purposes only and are not warranted for content, accuracy, or any other implied or explicit purpose.

This book is dedicated to my wife, Toni Marie Bacon. She is the love of my life.

People often remark that I'm pretty lucky. Luck is only important insofar as getting the chance to sell yourself at the right moment. After that, you've got to have talent and know how to use it.

Frank Sinatra

CONTENTS

Acknowledgments

I would first like to thank my wife and children for their support and confidence in me. My wife, Toni Bacon, worked side by side with me in our first retail hearing aid center, and she practices all of the Millionaire Selling Secrets found in this book.

Thanks also to Marie Quinn and Nyah Penney at our corporate headquarters for helping me pull this big project together.

I acknowledge the loving memory of my mother Marjorie Bacon—I am eternally grateful that she always encouraged me to pursue my goals and gave me the confidence to believe that I could actually achieve them.

And I also owe special thanks to my father Roger Bacon, who introduced me to the wonderful profession of selling and who taught me at an early age that the best helping hand I would ever get was at the end of my own arm!

ABOUT THE AUTHOR

Brett Bacon is a successful entrepreneur, attorney-at-law, veteran U.S. Army judge advocate general officer, business coach, speaker, and author.

He is CEO and president of Contract Vantage Advisory Group, Inc., and founder, CEO, and president of MyLife Franchise Corporation.

He earned his bachelor's degree from the University of New Hampshire in Political Science, his Juris Doctorate of Law degree from Vermont Law School, and his master of laws degree in Procurement Law from George Washington University. He also graduated from the U.S. Army Judge Advocate General's Law School Course at the University of Virginia. Brett continues his executive business education at Wharton's Graduate School of Business, University of Pennsylvania.

He lives in New Hampshire with his wife and children.

Brett is also coauthor of the book *Wake Up ... Live the Life You Love: In Service*. Coauthors include Steven E, Lee Beard, Brian Tracy, Dr. Wayne W. Dyer, and Ruben Gonzalez. From the best-selling series.

To learn more about Brett Bacon's speaking and business coaching services and to order additional copies of this book and his other books, e-books, and audio books, go to www.brettbacon.com.

This book is available at quantity discounts for bulk purchases. For more information, call 1-866-480-1220, or go to www.brettbacon.com.

The author can be reached at:

> Brett Bacon
> CEO and President
> Contract Vantage
> Advisory Group Corporation
> 101 Shattuck Way, Suite 4
> Newington, NH 03801
> Office: 603-431-1220
> Fax: 603-431-1104
> E-Mail: info@brettbacon.com
> Web site: www.brettbacon.com

PREFACE

I have personally sold millions of dollars of products and services, and I have coached others to do the same thing. I did this by applying the selling secrets of persuasion I am about to share with you in this book. I learned these Millionaire Selling Secrets from a combination of great mentors, formal education, trial and error, the school of hard knocks, and the lessons learned from thirty years of selling everything from life insurance to hearing aids. I am also an attorney-at-law, veteran U. S. Army judge advocate general officer, entrepreneur, author, speaker, and business coach. But no matter what I do, I am always selling—because I am always selling myself.

Selling is the art of persuasion, whether it is selling a product or service, presenting a new idea, or persuading someone to see your point of view.

I'm confident that you will enjoy this book and benefit from its secrets. Sir Francis Bacon famously said, "Some books are to be tasted, others to be swallowed, and some few to be chewed and digested." I hope that you chew and digest the lessons of this book—they will help to speed you on your way to becoming a millionaire!

INTRODUCTION

Money can't buy you happiness, but it does bring a more pleasant form of misery.
Mark Twain

Should *you* read this book? You should read this book immediately if you have the two following goals:

1. You want to be more persuasive in your work, and

2. You want to use these secrets of persuasion to help you become a millionaire.

So if you want to get your ideas across more effectively, help more people and become rich, then this book is for you!

In this book, I will share with you the ten most important Millionaire Selling Secrets. So what if you do not currently earn your living as a salesperson? It doesn't matter—this book is still for you! Selling applies to all types of communications and situations, not just sales presentations.

What can you expect to learn from this book? You will learn how to communicate more effectively, be more persuasive, and make more money in sales!

This book is broken down into the ten secrets, and after each secret there are Action Steps that you should put into practice before moving on to the next part. You should read and apply each secret in the chapter order of this book. Each secret is designed to build on the application of the secret before it.

The first Millionaire Selling Secret is the *secret of assuming your inevitable success.* I start with this secret because it is the foundation upon which all of the other secrets are built. You must assume that you will achieve your specific goals. If there is even a shadow of doubt in your mind, the other person will sense it instinctively and back away. After all, if you are not 100 percent committed to achieving your goals, why should anyone else be?

The second Millionaire Selling Secret is the *secret of building passion for what you do.* Building upon the assumption that you will get to where you want to go, you must possess passion for what you do. If you are passionate, then you truly have your skin in the game, and that is very powerful place to be.

The third Millionaire Selling Secret is the *secret of making a meaningful contribution to your customers.* In the process of selling yourself and your request, product, or service, you must find in your offer the contribution that you are making—both to your customer and society in general. This secret answers the question "What's in it for me?" At the same time, you must demonstrate to your customer that you can be trusted, that you have integrity.

The fourth Millionaire Selling Secret is the *secret of forging strong relationships with your customers.* You must establish a strong bond with your customer. Not only must you sell yourself, you must sell the relationship.

The fifth Millionaire Selling Secret is the *secret of asking questions to build your road map of persuasion.* You will learn to ask the right questions so that you can understand what is important to your customer, because until you discover what is really important to your customer, you cannot be persuasive at the highest possible level.

The sixth Millionaire Selling Secret is the *secret of embracing and loving objections.* This is one of my favorite secrets. You must embrace your customer's objections—objections give you the clues you need to understand your customer's needs.

The seventh Millionaire Selling Secret is the *secret of providing the best value for your customer.* You must offer a product or service that provides value to your customer. We all want the best and to pay as little as possible for it, right? Of course, this is not often realistic but it is a universal desire that you must address specifically in your presentation. I will show you how to find and sell the value in your presentation.

The eighth Millionaire Selling Secret is the *secret of agreeing with your customers.* This is another favorite selling secret of mine—and it is truly a well-kept secret if the argumentative style of the average salesperson is any indication! I can show you how to eliminate disagreement and confrontation from your sales presentations.

The ninth Millionaire Selling Secret is the *secret of advising your customers.* I learned this secret from the practice of law. You must be an adviser to your customers. After all, you are the expert on your product or service.

The tenth Millionaire Selling Secret is the *secret of role-playing.* In order for you to achieve in a short period of time the kind of incredible results that you desire, you must practice, practice, and practice some more. Role-playing is a special form of practice, and it must be done consistently throughout your selling career in order to achieve millionaire results.

So, roll up your sleeves and prepare to learn and apply these Millionaire Selling Secrets to your own life! You will be amazed at how quickly you can become more persuasive and effective with these simple, fast, and easy steps to make more money now!

SECRET ONE.
THE MILLIONAIRE SELLING SECRET OF *ASSUMING YOUR INEVITABLE SUCCESS*

CHAPTER 1
YOU ARE *ALWAYS* SELLING YOURSELF

If you don't sell, it's not the product that's wrong, it's you.

Estée Lauder

Whether you are aware of it or not, you are selling yourself from the moment you wake up in the morning to the moment you go to sleep, each and every day. There is no time off, no vacation days, no break from selling yourself. The only question is: What kind of selling job are you doing? Poor? Average? Outstanding?

Let's start with some definitions, so that we are on the same page. Millionaire Selling is an incredible system of persuasion that you can apply to any business situation. *Millionaire Selling is putting your best foot forward at all times.* You must exude confidence, passion, and compassion. Millionaire Selling is not about getting what you want at the expense of others. But it *is* about getting your point across in the most effective way possible and helping others get what *they* want. When you advocate something that is good for others, then it will be good for you as well.

So what if you are not paid as a salesperson at this time? Can this book help you? Absolutely! I don't care what job you have; selling is involved. Selling is persuading, and you must be persuasive to be successful, no matter what the job—unless you live on a deserted island!

Good selling is not about being phony or insincere. It is just the opposite. Millionaire Selling is about being true to yourself and true to others. And if

3

what you offer to your customers is good for them, then you will find the road to becoming a millionaire will open up before you in surprising ways as you begin your journey toward greater influence and wealth.

ACTION STEPS

1. Make a list of all the situations in your job where you would like to be able to communicate more effectively. Next to each situation, write down the specific objectives that you would like to accomplish.

2. Make a list of all of the people that you would like to be able to persuade and influence in your work, from customers to co-workers to supervisors to suppliers. For each group, write down the objectives that you would like to accomplish through persuasive communications.

3. As you go through this book, think about your list of situations and people that you want to influence, and make notes after each chapter of how you can apply each Millionaire Selling Secret to your particular circumstances. This is an important technique. You are training your mind to focus on the specifics, not general situations that don't apply to your customer.

4. Go to www.brettbacon.com for additional tools and information on how to sell yourself better.

CHAPTER 2
YOU *MUST* ASSUME THE SALE

There is no such thing as "soft sell" and "hard sell." There is only "smart sell" and "stupid sell."

Charles Brower

What do I mean when I say "assume the sale"? I mean that even before you meet your customer, you imagine how the entire successful presentation will go—from the introduction to shaking hands—and in your mind's eye, your presentation always ends the same way: you get the sale. At all times, your focus must be on your customer and the benefits that your customer will enjoy after the sale.

Your confidence must be absolutely unshakeable. It is okay to feel a little fear—Winston Churchill once said that courage is not the absence of fear. It is taking action in spite of the fear that counts.

Your selling confidence must be built up brick by brick. The bricks of confidence are: (1) you know yourself and you know that you must first and foremost sell yourself before you can sell your product or service; (2) you know your product or service frontward and backward; and (3) you know that your product or service will help your customer to live a better life.

When you assume the sale to the marrow of your bones, amazing things start to happen—your customer senses your confidence and is reassured by it.

ACTION STEPS

1. Think about all of the situations and people that you want to persuade—and assume that you will achieve your goals. Create vivid pictures in your mind: your customer agrees to buy, you are recognized and rewarded by your company for your sales, and your family benefits from the money that you make from your increased sales.

2. Don't be your own worst critic. Develop a thick skin to critics who question your ability to achieve your goals. Assume that you will accomplish your goals and keep imagining how good it will feel when you do. Don't get discouraged by temporary setbacks. Keep moving forward!

3. Go to www.brettbacon.com for additional tools and information on how to assume the sale.

CHAPTER 3
YOU MUST ASSUME YOU *WILL* BECOME A MILLIONAIRE

Nothing can resist a human will that will stake even its existence on its purpose.

Benjamin Disraeli

They conquer who believe they can.

Ralph Waldo Emerson

When I use the word assume, I don't mean a wish or hope. Everybody hopes to be a millionaire someday. In my experience, "someday" is the excuse we tell ourselves to put off taking action today.

You must turn your wish to become a millionaire into a must to become a millionaire. In my 2009 book *Wake Up ... Live the Life You Love: In Service*, I reveal how you can build your own must-do list of success. The world is full of dreamers. For most of my life, I dreamed of becoming a millionaire like so many others. But my life did not change dramatically until I made the shift from dreaming and wishing to a must-do mentality.

Your personal list of musts that leads you down the path to becoming a millionaire must have, at its core, your personal list of the whys behind the musts. Why you want to become a millionaire is up to you. Start writing down the whys and the musts will inevitably follow. The key to a powerful why is to find something bigger than yourself—for example, achieving financial security for your family, getting the best education for your children, making a lasting contribution to the world, helping your customers, etc.

Take a clean piece of paper. Draw a line down the middle of the paper from top to bottom. On the left side at the top of the paper, write the heading Whys, and on the right side of the paper, write the heading Musts. Start with your list of whys. If you list under whys "to live a long life so that I can be there for my family," then on the right column, across from the why column, list all of the musts that you will accomplish in order to achieve the ultimate why of living a long and healthy life. For example, you could list "lose ten pounds over the next twelve months—final weigh-in on December 31." Your must list needs to be very specific. If your must is not specific, then it is just a dream or a wish, which is definitely not going to lead you to achieving your why. In this case, if you simply write "lose weight," you are not making the must specific enough—when, how, and under what circumstances?

Your musts have to be measurable. In order to know if you are moving ahead toward your musts, you will need to be able to score your progress. Once you have your general why and must lists completed, review them and begin to break them down into separate parts that stand alone.

Your assumption that you will become a millionaire will only be as strong as your commitment to written, specific, measureable must-do steps. And you'll need to have a timetable. Timetables are tricky things—they must be ambitious in order to get you moving and to keep your excitement level high—but on the other hand, your timetable cannot be so outrageously short that even you do not believe it. The key here is not whether anyone else thinks you can do it. What really counts is whether you believe it. And make sure that your timetable is not so long that there is no sense of urgency to it.

For example, you could set a timetable to become a millionaire over a seven-year period. Then break down on your must-do list what you need to accomplish in year one, year two, etc., leading to the achievement of your millionaire must-do by the end of year seven. You should put a great deal of thought into how you will achieve each step—and be very specific.

In addition to putting your must-do list in writing and making it specific and measurable, you need to review your must-do list every day! Carry in your pocket a laminated card about the size of a credit card with your own personal must-do list for the calendar year. Then refer to it every day. Why? Because we live in a fast-paced world of changes and distractions, and it is too easy to get sidetracked and forget your must-do list if you do not refer to it on a daily basis.

When you refer to your must-do list every day, you will not lose track of your objectives—and your mind will work both consciously and subconsciously on taking the daily steps toward you achieving your millionaire status.

So what happens if you fall short of your must-do timetable? Take stock of what went right and what went wrong. Do more of what went right, and do less of what went wrong. Sounds simple, doesn't it? It is simple to understand but not so simple to do, unless you keep your eye on the prize on a daily basis. That is why it is so critical to review your must-do list daily and make changes to your list, including specific musts and timetables as necessary in real time, not six months after the fact.

If you stick to the daily review of your millionaire must-do list for a week, then you can do it for two weeks—then a month, then a quarter, then a year. You will have increased confidence and resolve to stick to your must-do plan because you will know what your plan is and how to get there. It is your own personal road map, with GPS capability. If you run a little off course, just like GPS in your car, your must-do road map will redirect you back on course.

So take the following millionaire must-do Action Steps below to build your own road map to millionaire success.

ACTION STEPS

1. Write out your Why List on the left side of a two column piece of paper. Write out your Must-Do List on the right hand column.

2. Print the ten key headings of your annual millionaire must-do list on a credit card-sized piece of paper, laminate it, and keep in your pocket for daily review.

3. Review your master Must-Do Action Plan on a monthly basis, make revisions, and add new must-dos as you go.

4. Share your Must-Do Action Plan with your family and friends. They will share your excitement and spur you on to greater achievement. This will also tap into your desire to keep your word—to yourself!

5. Go to www.brettbacon.com for additional tools and information on how to build your Must-Do Action Plan.

SECRET TWO.
THE MILLIONAIRE SELLING
SECRET OF *BUILDING*
PASSION FOR WHAT YOU DO

CHAPTER 4
FIND PASSION FOR WHAT YOU SELL!

Clarity of mind means clarity of passion, too; this is why a great mind loves ardently and see distinctively what he loves.

Blais Pascal

You must have passion for what you do. More specifically, you must have passion for what you *sell*. Secret Two is broken down into five key parts: (1) *finding* the passion for what you sell, (2) *showing* your passion to your customers, (3) creating your sales mantra to maintain your passion, (4) realizing the benefits of passion to your work, and (5) bringing it all together.

Finding the passion in what you sell may be easier said than done. In my case, finding passion for our products and services was easy for me. One of our companies, for example, offers hearing aid products and services to the hearing impaired. I am passionate about helping our patients to hear better so that they can live better.

So where is the passion in your product or service? Let's suppose that you sell newspaper advertising space to small businesses in your community. On its surface, this may seem to be a service that is difficult to feel passionate about. But let's take a closer look. Small business advertising is a critical part of making a small business a success. And small business is the backbone of the American economy. Small businesses provide vital products and services to the community. Small businesses provide jobs and income to both owners and employees. These are all things that you can be very passionate about! You are making an important contribution to your community and the economy when you sell advertising to your small business customers.

Now take a closer look at your particular product or service. Ask yourself the following questions to find the passion in your work:

- How will my product or service improve the lives of my customers?

- How do I add value for my customers?

- What is unique about what I offer that I can be truly proud of?

Follow the additional Action Steps below to find the passion in what you sell!

ACTION STEPS

1. Write down all of the things that your customers get when they own your product or service. Identify all of the features and matching benefits to your customers. What is it about the benefits that create passion for what you do?

2. Share your passion with your friends and family.

3. Go to www.brettbacon.com for additional tools and information on how to build passion for your work.

CHAPTER 5
YOUR PASSION MUST SHOW!
HOW YOU SAY IT IS MORE
IMPORTANT THAN *WHAT*
YOU SAY

You have to have your heart in the business and the business in your heart.

Thomas J. Watson, Sr.

Now that you have identified what gets you excited about what you sell, you must show it to your customer! You will immediately stand out from the crowd if you master this Millionaire Selling Secret. The key here is to *show* your customer that you are passionate. If your customer has to guess about your level of interest and commitment to your product or service, you are not going to succeed as much as you are capable of.

You must realize that your customer is buying *you* first, and then your product or service second. In large part, the customer's decision to buy from you is based on their sense of your passion for your product or service. After all, if you are not passionate about what you do, why should the customer spend their dollars on what you sell?

So how do you show your passion? It starts with your body posture. Do you express energy and excitement in your posture and body movement? This can be very powerful. For example, we train our employees to get out from behind the counter and walk up to and personally greet each and every patient who walks in the door of one of our hearing centers. Our patients are pleasantly surprised by this small but important gesture. When is the last time anyone got up out of their chair in a health care center to greet you? How about in a retail store? I bet it's difficult to recall a single example. Actions speak louder than words—and the action of getting up and walking up to your customer in a relaxed and friendly manner speaks volumes to the customer.

Your voice is a critical measure of your passion and is one of the most neglected areas I find when observing sales presentations. Does your voice sound engaging and exciting? Or is it dull and non-expressive? Psychologists tell us that the pitch and pace of your voice has an enormous impact on people, so you must be aware of *how* you say *everything* to the customer.

Eye contact is another critical way to show your passion. If you are not committed enough to look your customer in the eyes then you need to go back to the drawing board to find your passion.

Your dress and appearance must show your passion as well. Are you dressed appropriately for the part? I believe that you should always be dressed slightly better than your average customer. In our hearing company, for example, all of our hearing specialists wear crisp, white lab coats with their names and titles clearly embroidered on their pockets. I am shocked and surprised by the current casual trend in health care and retail in general. I don't want my doctor to be dressed in jeans and a T-shirt when I am getting a checkup. So dress appropriately for the job.

You will read in more detail in a later chapter of this book that you should see yourself as a personal adviser to your customer, and you should be sure to dress in a way that supports your passion and role as an adviser who wants to be taken seriously.

Passion for your product or service also means being proficient during the demonstration of your product. This should go without saying, but I have seen enough mistakes in this area to convince me that it is worth emphasizing. In the later chapter on role-playing, I will show you how to practice with a partner so that you can smoothly and flawlessly demonstrate all of features of your particular product or service.

ACTION STEPS

1. Write out a list of all of the ways in which you can express your passion during the presentation. Start with your voice, facial expressions, eye contact, and body posture.

2. Create a video of your sales presentation in a role-play with a co-worker, family member, or friend. Ask the person role-playing the customer to be as realistic as possible. Review the video and pay special attention to your voice inflection, your mannerisms, and your expressions. Identify what works and what does not. Look for additional ways to express your passion to the customer.

3. Go to www.brettbacon.com for additional tools and information on how to show the passion that you feel for your product or service.

CHAPTER 6
DEVELOP YOUR SALES MANTRA

Confidence is that feeling by which the mind embarks in great and honorable courses with a sure hope and trust in itself.

Marcus Cicero

Now that you have discovered the passion in your work and you know how to express your passion to your customer, you need one additional critical tool to ensure that you keep your passion pumped up for each and every customer. One of the best ways I have discovered to maintain peak passion throughout the day is to repeat my own personal sales mantra before meeting each customer.

For example, in one of our companies, our mission is to test hearing and to help our patients hear better through the use of hearing instruments. So we teach our employees to repeat the following mantra to themselves before they see each and every patient: "I am going to help my patient hear better today!"

This sounds simple, and it is—most great ideas are simple. So look at your product and service and create your own sales mantra. A great sales mantra must be short and sweet and express the essence of what you what to accomplish for your customer—it is the essence of why you are so passionate about your job.

For example, if you sell shoes, your mantra might be "I am going to help my customer find the best shoes today!"

A great mantra must also have a sense of urgency about it. I always like to include the time frame for the customer to make a decision; in most cases, it is today. If you don't have a sense of urgency, your customer certainly will not.

Once you have your mantra memorized, you must say it to yourself throughout the day. The key to the effectiveness of a great sales mantra is repetition, so repeat it to yourself constantly throughout the day to stay focused and to keep your passion high!

ACTION STEPS

1. Write down all of the benefits of your product or service. Look at your product or service through the eyes of the customer. Ask "What is in it for me?" The answer to that question is your mantra.

2. Start repeating your mantra throughout the day. It must be simple, short, and capture the essence of why you are passionate about your work—to help your customers in your own unique way.

3. As you begin to use your mantra, don't be afraid to revise it, streamline it, and sharpen it until it feels just right. Now say it to yourself out loud. There is something about the mind-body connection that requires actually saying it and not just thinking it.

4. Go to www.brettbacon.com for additional tools and information on developing your sales mantra.

CHAPTER 7
PASSION MAKES HARD
WORK FEEL EASY!

Opportunity is missed by most people because it is dressed in overalls and looks like work.

Thomas A. Edison

Passion makes work *seem* easy. When you are passionate about your work, the day goes by much faster, and you are happy about the contribution that you make to your customers and your community

This is one of the great benefits of finding passion in what you do. Not only will it make you more persuasive, the actual work will *feel* easier! When I train students, they often say in response, "But there are some things that I hate doing that are required in my job, like the paperwork that I have to fill out. How can I feel passionate about that!"

The short answer is, if you only focus on the parts or your work that you hate, eventually you will forget about the passion that you have for what you do and all of the work you do will soon feel like pure drudgery!

That is why you must clearly identify all of the things that you can feel passionate about and then focus on how you are improving the lives of your customers. By focusing on what you are passionate about, you will have an easier time pushing through the parts of your work that are hard to feel excited about—such as filling out paperwork.

And don't forget about your sales mantra. Not only does your mantra come in handy when you are getting yourself pumped up before you meet your customer, your mantra helps you when you are tackling some of the important but tough tasks required to get the job done—like paperwork.

As Thomas Edison said, opportunity is missed by most people because it looks like work. But you are not going to miss the opportunities in your sales career—especially the opportunity to sell yourself—because you are going to focus on what makes you passionate! Your focus on passion will make the opportunity and the work that goes into it *feel* better.

So never forget your passion, especially during the tough parts of your day, and you will find it easier to tackle the necessary tasks that you must do to seize the opportunities before you.

ACTION STEPS

1. Identify all of the essential tasks that you must do each day in order to get the job done—even the tasks that you do not like and would like to avoid. Now focus throughout the day on the tasks that you feel passionate about, and understand that you must still complete the essential tasks that you do not enjoy in order to get to the tasks that you do enjoy.

2. Identify any tasks that you do not like that you are now doing that are not required or essential to get the job done or are somebody else's job. Then eliminate these tasks from your daily routine. If you are truly honest with yourself, you will find some tasks that you can drop from your daily routine altogether. This will give you more time and energy to focus on essential, important tasks that truly help you to fulfill your passion.

3. Go to www.brettbacon.com for additional tools and information on how to build passion for what you sell.

CHAPTER 8
PASSION EQUALS PERSUASION

And Jesus said to them, 'Follow Me, and I will make you become fishers of men.'

Mark 1:17

Passion equals persuasion because you are giving your heart to the customers—and your customers will give you their heart in return. Emotions are so critical to being persuasive, and they are often ignored in today's business world and in traditional selling techniques.

There is a general, mistaken, overemphasis on the role of logic in being persuasive and in sales training in general. Don't get me wrong—logic plays an important role. But as we build the Millionaire Selling Secret Pyramid of Persuasion, the foundation of the pyramid is to win the heart.

This key Millionaire Selling Secret is worth repeating: **win the *heart* of your customer *first*.**

And you win the heart of your customer first by showing your unwavering passion first.

Passion is so rare in today's business world. We are taught to be logical and boring in our presentations. Logic is just one part of being persuasive—and it is not the most important part. However, it is intoxicating to the customer to encounter a truly passionate salesperson. If you are truly passionate, you will be more persuasive.

And if your passion shows, you will win the hearts of your customers. Their minds will surely follow.

I am an avid fly fisherman. When I first started to learn fly fishing, it was all about me and what I wanted to get—namely lots of fish. But I soon learned that I had to focus exclusively on what the fish wants, not what I want. Then I started to see incredible results.

Fly fishing requires absolute focus and attention. If you take your attention off of your fly for just a moment, you will miss the opportunity to hook the fish and the fish will spit out the imitation fly in a fraction of a second.

Fly fishing is a lot like selling: you must focus on what your customer wants, you must maintain your focus at all times, and you must offer something that is attractive to your customer. You must show them the passion that you feel, and that passion must be firmly anchored in the benefits that you bring to your customer.

And you must never give up. If you do not succeed with a particular customer, then move on to the next opportunity and do not allow your passion to drop.

You are selling yourself, and you must be a fisher of men—you must first attract them to you, and then to your product or service. If you can do this, then you can sell anything. Passion equals persuasion.

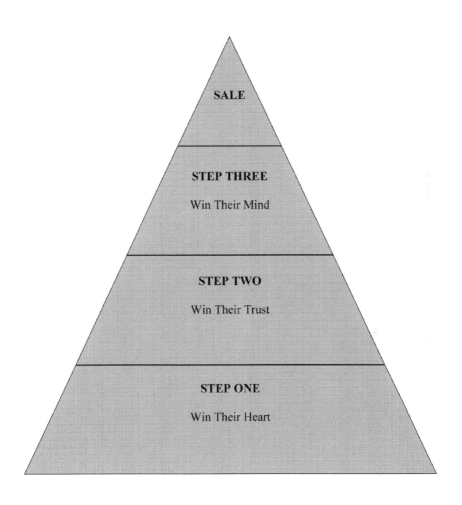

The Millionaire Selling Secrets Pyramid of Persuasion

ACTION STEPS

1. Your passion is what makes you unique to your customer. Identify all of the elements of your passion that make you unique—how you talk, act, move; what you say; what you do; how you listen; what you feel; and what you think about when you are presenting your product or service to your customer. This bundle of traits is what makes you truly unique in the eye of your customer—it is the essence of what makes you persuasive. You attract customers to your point of view and your offering when you show them all of the traits of your passion.

2. Go to www.brettbacon.com for additional tools and information on how to show your passion to your customers.

SECRET THREE.
THE MILLIONAIRE SELLING SECRET OF *MAKING A MEANINGFUL CONTRIBUTION TO YOUR CUSTOMERS*

CHAPTER 9
FOCUS ON WHAT YOU CAN DO FOR YOUR CUSTOMERS

If we do not lay out ourselves in the service of mankind, whom should we serve?

John Adams

Now that you have identified the passion behind what you sell, you must focus that passion like a laser beam on the one thing that your customer is always thinking: "What is in it for me?"

It is only through clearly answering this question in the customer's mind that you truly make a meaningful contribution to your customers. And it is meaningful because your customer understands, at the end of your presentation and at the end of the sale, that you are absolutely focused on their needs, not yours.

The most common mistake that I see in new and experienced salespeople alike is an obvious focus on what is in it for them, as the salespeople. An experienced salesperson often tries to justify this mistake by his overall sales results. The fact that you can get some sales by focusing on your own needs rather than those of the customer does not prove that it is the right approach.

If you are an experienced salesperson, do you repeatedly tell your customer what *you* need to get out of the sale, in terms of dollars, quantity, terms, etc? Do you tell your customer that you are going to be in trouble with management if you do not charge a certain amount, provide a certain warranty with limitations, etc? If so, you are definitely putting the cart before the horse. Essentially, you are asking your customer to think in a way that is contrary to his own self-interest.

While it is true that your typical customer understands that you are going to receive some benefits from the transaction, you don't have to rub his nose in it. My point is that you will get *better* sales results and you will be *more* persuasive if you focus solely on what is good for your customer, not what is good for you. Your rewards come after the sale.

This is big part of the persuasive power of the Millionaire Selling Secrets— you must combine the passion (heart) for what you do with your laser focus on what benefits the customer, not you.

Put yourself in the shoes of your customers. What are the benefits that they want in your product or service? What are their concerns that you must address? How are you improving their lives and society in general by offering your product or service?

Why am I referring to the benefits to society in general? Because no person is an island. You need to think beyond the immediate benefits to the customer and expand your list of benefits to society. If you don't think this part through, you are missing a very powerful opportunity to show your customer that the benefits of your product or service reach far beyond the immediate benefits to him. Your customer may or may not be aware of the more general benefits to society. It is your job to spell out these broader benefits to the customer.

And for some customers, this is the most persuasive part of your presentation. For example, if you are selling gas-efficient cars and you only talk about the immediate benefit to the customer (savings in gas), you are not being as persuasive and helpful to the customer as you can. What about the benefits to society? You will be cutting down on pollution and global warming by increasing gas mileage, just to name two.

On the other hand, it is reckless to only talk about the benefits to society. If you only talk about global warming with the customer, he may miss the point that there are some personal benefits to be enjoyed, too—such as fewer trips to the gas pump!

ACTION STEPS

1. Write out an outline of your entire sales presentation, from the moment that you meet your customer (greeting), to the demonstration of your product or service, to the close of the sale.

2. Now highlight every single thing that you say or do that answers the question for the customer "What is in it for me?"

3. When answering the customer's question, "What is in it for me?" make sure to list two columns of benefits: those personal to the customer and those to society in general.

4. Identify and ruthlessly remove anything from your sales presentation that would answer the question "What is in it for me, the salesperson?"

5. Go to www.brettbacon.com for additional tools and information on how to stay focused on your customer's benefits during your sales presentation.

CHAPTER 10
YOUR INTEGRITY MUST SHOW

If you find it in your heart to care for somebody else, you will have succeeded.

Maya Angelou

In order to make a meaningful contribution to your customer, as discussed in the previous chapter, you must focus exclusively on what benefits the customer and society in general. And you must demonstrate to your customer that you are worthy of trust.

If every benefit that you point out is true, but your customer does not trust you, you will not be persuasive and you will not help the customer.

Your customer's trust in you is a very fragile thing. Some customers have been burned by other salespeople so many times in the past that they will not trust you at all in the beginning, and you must build and earn their trust. Other customers will give you some trust up front, and it is yours to lose or keep.

So how do you earn their trust? The short answer is by doing what you say and saying what you do. Don't overpromise what can be done or exaggerate the benefits. Your customers will remember everything that you say and do.

So how do you lose their trust? In my experience coaching salespeople, it is the little things that come back to haunt you: not sending the e-mail that you promised, not returning the call on time, not mailing out the sales materials when promised, etc. These little mistakes can begin to add up in the mind of the customer: "If I can't trust him to follow through on the little things, what happens when I have a big problem?"

Often, the real problem behind missed deadlines and follow-through is poor organization and time management. People in general are pretty forgiving about an isolated incident of dropping the ball, such as a late follow-up e-mail, but if the customer sees a pattern of broken promises, small or large, you will lose that customer sooner or later. And what will you lose? Current and future sales will be lost, along with customer referrals—one of the most powerful secrets to selling more in less time.

When you miss a commitment—and you will—make sure to accept responsibility, apologize to the customer, and fix the problem. Your customer understands that you are human and not perfect—as long as you admit the mistake without excuses. Excuses are the death of integrity. If you focus on making excuses to your customers for your shortcomings, you are not being professional and you are certainly not being persuasive.

ACTION STEPS

1. Write down every single commitment that you make to prospects and customers over the next week.

2. The following week, review all of your commitments from the previous week. Did you meet all of your short-term commitments, and are you on track to meet your long-term commitments?

3. Call all of your prospects and customers who you have not spoken to in a while. Let them know that you care and you are ready to help them whenever they need it.

4. If you drop the ball and miss a commitment, don't pretend it didn't happen and hope that your customer will forget. Admit the mistake—small or large—and apologize. Make sure that you have the solution ready with the apology. Customers want to know that you are going to take responsibility for your actions. This is the foundation of integrity.

5. Go to www.brettbacon.com for additional tools and information on how to build your integrity in the sales process.

SECRET FOUR.
THE MILLIONAIRE SELLING SECRET OF *BUILDING STRONG RELATIONSHIPS WITH YOUR CUSTOMERS*

CHAPTER 11
YOUR GOAL IS TO ESTABLISH AND MAINTAIN LONG-TERM RELATIONSHIPS WITH YOUR CUSTOMERS

Our business is about technology, yes. But it's also about operations and customer relationships.

Michael Dell

You are in the business of building and maintaining long-term relationships with your customers. If you are doing your job right, your customers won't dream of buying from anyone else.

This is a critical Millionaire Selling Secret—you are selling the *relationship* between you and your customer, first and foremost. It is not the product, not the technology, not the bells and whistles that come with your product or service that are most important. After all, if it is only about the product or service, your customer can likely find the same somewhere else.

If you are not building strong, long-term relationships with your customers, you are starting from scratch every day. You must continuously find new customers to sell to, because you are not building a foundation of customers who will come back to you again and again and refer other customers to you.

Who would you rather sell to? Someone you already know and have a good relationship with or a complete stranger? And when you meet a new customer, which would you rather have, a complete stranger or someone who was referred to you by one of your customers with a glowing recommendation?

Thinking long-term is a critical part of Millionaire Selling Secrets. When you meet a new customer, you are not in for the short-term sale. While important, the immediate sale is just the first step on a long journey. If you are thinking about the long-term well-being of the customer, you will not only take care of his immediate needs, but you will have a customer and friend for life. You will also build a book of business from new sales and referrals that will make your future bright.

So what happens if you change companies, products, or services? If you have a strong, long-term relationship with your customers, they will go with you to your new product or service. However, if you did not build lasting relationships with your customers, then you are always starting from scratch.

The secret to building long-term relationships is showing your customers how much you care. And you show your customers how much you care by proving that you are going to be there for them for the long haul, not just for that one sale.

So let's assume that you have made your first sale with a particular customer, and you want to build a long-term relationship that will last through the ups and downs of the economy, changes in jobs, and changes in the customer's definition of "What's in it for me?" Now what?

Since you have passion for what you do, and for the benefits that you provide to your customer, it is easy to be creative and think of many ways to build that bridge from today's sale to future sales.

First there is the follow-up. Even if there is no requirement or necessity to make the follow-up phone call, that is all the more reason to do it. This sometimes takes a bit of courage, depending on what you are selling, because you might hear objections and complaints from the customer. But you have to be willing to deal with that—it gives you an opportunity to show to your customers that you really care and that you will help them with their problems.

You must change your thinking from being *reactive* with customers to being *proactive* with customers. In the case of the follow-up call, you are definitely being proactive by making the call first. If your customer is happy with the product or service, he will be pleased to know that you care enough to call to see how he is doing, even though you didn't have to. And if the customer is unhappy, the fact that you called him first often takes the full force out of his complaint.

Another key way to building long-term relationships is to stay in touch with your customers. I find this is often missed by new and experienced salespeople alike—they just forget about their customers after the sale. And I have heard all of the excuses: "I don't have the time" or "I don't get paid to see how my customers are doing."

I think these two excuses fall flat for two reasons. First, if you are not taking the time to follow up with your customers, then you are creating *more* work for yourself, not less. If you don't stay in touch with your customers, little problems can soon become big problems. And happy customers will appreciate your follow-up.

As for the second excuse of not getting paid for follow-up—actually you *do* get paid for it, but just not today. If you are working on a full-commission basis, it is true that you will not be paid *yet* for making the follow-up call, but you will not be paid *later* in the form of additional sales and referrals.

Then there is the power of *thank you*. If you want to separate yourself from the vast majority of salespeople, send a thank-you card. Your customer will appreciate your thoughtfulness, and it requires little effort on your part. You will stand out in the crowd, because very few salespeople bother to follow up with a thank you.

In our retail companies, we always follow the sale with a personalized thank-you card. The card itself has our company name on it, along with a photo of the sales and service team. There is room in the card for a personal note, which you should always take time to write.

If your company already has thank-you cards gathering dust in a closet, take them out and use them consistently with all of your customers—not just your favorites. I have found over the years that some of my very best long-term customers started out as difficult, suspicious, and demanding. But once I won their trust, they became our most loyal customers. If your company does not have thank-you cards, you need to buy your own personal set.

Taking the long view will also help you to keep things in perspective when you are having a bad sales day, which happens to all of us. If you are thinking long-term, not just about your customers but also about your goals and objectives, then you are less likely to overreact to today's problems. And if you do not overreact as much, you will be more receptive to your customers and less likely to miss the sale because you are having a bad day.

Another easy way to maintain long-term relationships is to send birthday and holiday cards to your customers. This is a nice personal touch that will make you feel good, and I guarantee your customers will appreciate it. This is another opportunity for you to stand out from the crowd. You may sell a product or service that is widely available to the customer—but you are unique. Give the customer as many reasons as possible to do business with you and not the competition.

ACTION STEPS

1. Identify all of the follow-up steps that you can take after the first sale. The follow-up call, thank-you cards, birthday cards, holiday cards, invitations to new product events, new catalog offerings, lunch and learn events, etc.

2. Build a database of your customers' names and contact information.

3. Think long-term. Don't drop a customer from your holiday card list just because they haven't purchased from you lately. The next sale may be just around the corner—don't lose it because you decided it was not worth keeping in contact.

4. Go to www.brettbacon.com for additional tools and information on how to build and keep strong relationships with your customers.

CHAPTER 12
OBSERVE CUSTOMER'S MANNER OF SPEECH AND GESTURES AND MATCH THEM

If you can walk with kings, but never lose the common touch.

From the poem "If" by Rudyard Kipling

Your powers of observation during your face-to-face meeting will be put to the test with every customer. If you pay close attention to your customer's manner of speech and gestures, and then you match them, you dramatically increase your ability to persuade. If you do not, you will dramatically reduce your ability to persuade.

It is a basic fact of human psychology that we relate more easily to people who are similar to us. And by closely observing and matching the manner of speech and gestures of your customer, you are helping him to be more receptive to your presentation. I am not asking you to change who you are—just your style of communication.

Listen to and observe very carefully your customer, beginning with the greeting. Is the customer shy, outgoing, friendly, reserved? Don't be too quick to rush to the customer and pump his hand with a powerful handshake. Give your customer a moment to see you before you step forward. You should always smile, but not too much at first.

Listen very carefully to the type of words that the customer uses. It will give you enormous clues as to what is most important to him and whether he uses feelings or logic in his decision-making process. For example, if your customer says, "I feel that I would like to get a new computer," you are probably dealing with a customer who makes decisions based on his feelings. You can match this style of speech by saying something like, "I know how you feel. Perhaps this model is something you would like."

On the other hand, if the customer likes to think that logic rules his decisions, look for clues like, "I think that the most reasonable type of snow tire for me is ..." You might say, "It is obvious that you have put a lot of thought into this. Let's find the most logical choice for you."

Listen very carefully for your customer's volume and pace of speech. Does he speak slowly and softly? Then you should start this way. Does he speak loudly and quickly? Then you should match his volume and pace of speech.

Does your customer move quickly and use many hand gestures? If so, try to match him in style and intensity. Look carefully at the distance between you and your customer if you meet for the first time standing up. You should not stand too close—this might be viewed as threatening or intimidating. And if you find that your customer makes an adjustment to stand closer or farther away from you, it is probably a good indication of the distance that he feels most comfortable with.

After you have spent a few minutes with the customer and he appears more comfortable with you, you will be able to adjust your speech and gestures. The contrast can be used to emphasize certain key points. For example, if you have been talking in a low volume for a few minutes, you may want to raise your voice slightly to make a key point. This volume change will be noticed by your customer, and it can be very effective.

Another example would be a fast-talking customer. If your speech is initially fast to match his, you may want to slow down your speech for the special emphasis of key points.

Note that this chapter is about the style of communication, not necessarily the substance. In other words, even though you may be dealing with a customer who thinks that he makes all buying decisions logically and communicates that way, that does not mean that he doesn't put his feelings first in the buying decision, which I believe to be the case with most people— even with the logical thinker. Logic has its place in the selling process, but generally speaking, not at the beginning of the sales process.

Most people make a buying decision first with their hearts or emotions and then decide if they can trust you. Then they justify the decision with logic.

The problem is, amateur salespeople try to bury the customer with logic and technical specifications right out of the gate, and this can kill the sale and their opportunity to help the customer.

Never talk over the head of your customer. What I mean by that is never use terms and words that average person would find confusing. The selling environment is no place to demonstrate how many words, abbreviations, and acronyms that you can use that no one knows—especially your customer. Save that for Scrabble! As obvious as this might seem, I am willing to *bet* that you are peppering your sales presentation *right now* with words that the average person, who is not specifically trained in your product or service, has absolutely no clue about.

A confused mind cannot make a decision. Your job is to be persuasive, to speak and communicate in a way that makes sense to your customer. If you confuse your customer with techno-jargon or specialized terms, you will get a fraction of the number of sales that you could by speaking in plain English.

But don't get me wrong, I am not talking about dumbing down your presentation. It takes a lot of work to eliminate the confusing words in your presentation—after all, you want to show off your expertise, right? Wrong! Show off by speaking clearly and in plain, simple English!

ACTION STEPS

1. Write down, word for word, your typical presentation. Show it to a family member or friend and have him point out every word that he doesn't understand. If this is going to be effective, your friend can't be familiar with the specialized terminology of your business.

2. Replace all confusing words with plain English words.

3. Keep a notepad nearby, and after every presentation with a customer, write down the words that you used that need to be replaced with plain English. This will take some time, especially if you have been in the habit of using industry terms for some time.

4. When role-playing your presentation with colleagues or family members, ask them to flag any words that are not plain English. See Section 10 of this book about role-playing.

5. Go to www.brettbacon.com for additional tools and information on how to improve the words that you use during your sales presentations.

CHAPTER 13
YOUR CUSTOMERS ARE YOUR ULTIMATE SOURCE OF BUSINESS REFERRALS

You can make more friends in two months by becoming interested in other people than you can in two years by trying to get other people interested in you.

Dale Carnegie

Once you have a customer, you want to keep him for life. And you want your customers to be your ultimate source of business referrals. If you have followed the Millionaire Selling Secrets, you will have an ever-growing base of satisfied customers sending you new customers.

There are a few simple steps that you can take to dramatically increase the number of referrals. The first step is to *ask for referrals*. If one definition of a secret is that it is not commonly known or practiced, then this step is definitely a secret, because in my experience as both a sales coach and a customer, this simple technique is rarely used.

At the end of every presentation, whether you make the sale or not, ask for referrals. That's right—even if you don't make the sale, you should ask for a referral! Just because your customer does not buy from you today does not mean that he will not buy from you tomorrow! So why waste an opportunity to ask for a referral? The sales profession is in part a numbers game—you have to see enough prospects in order to have a certain percentage of customers. Don't tie your own hands by failing to take this important step.

If your presentation results in a sale, then so much the better—ask for a referral. We train our employees in one of our health care companies to say something like this after every sale: "Can I ask for your help? I know that your family and friends respect your opinion, and if they have a hearing problem, they would certainly appreciate your recommendation. If you feel that we have taken great care of your hearing needs, I would personally appreciate it if you would recommend your friends and family to our practice. We are accepting new patients at this time, so we certainly appreciate your recommendation."

Pretty simple, right? And very powerful! Make sure to ask your customer personally—don't have the front desk person do this by mail. Look your customer straight in the eye and ask for his help. Most people want to be helpful, and you shouldn't be too proud to ask for it. You want to time your request for help when the customer is feeling happy about you and your service or product.

The second step is to show your appreciation to customers who do in fact give referrals. This can be done in the form of a small gift or gift certificate. At a minimum, you should send a thank-you card. You should also build a referral program. Tell your customers that for every referral that you get, they will receive a gift of some type that is appropriate to your product or service and the amount of the sale.

The third step is to keep asking for referrals from your customers—long after the initial sale. You should be in constant contact with your customers, and during the course of your long-term relationships, you will have many opportunities to ask for referrals. And if you ask in a pleasant and professional way, your customers will not object.

ACTION STEPS

1. Practice your referral request and always ask for referrals of all customers that you meet—whether you make the sale or not.

2. Show your appreciation for your referrals by giving the customer a gift that is appropriate to the referral sale.

3. Create your own referral rewards program. Encourage your customers to take advantage of the gifts and benefits of referrals. Offer something free or give away dinner coupons from a local restaurant. Prepare a basic referral card or flyer with several tear-out business cards with

your name on one side and a space for your customer's name on the other side.

4. Keep asking for referrals every time you see your customer. Remember you are in this for the long haul—first for your customer and second for your livelihood!

5. Go to www.brettbacon.com for additional tools and information on how to build your customer referrals.

SECRET FIVE.
The Millionaire Selling Secret of *Asking Questions to Build Your Road Map of Persuasion*

CHAPTER 14
ASK QUESTIONS ABOUT THEIR NEEDS AND WANTS

He who asks a question is a fool for five minutes; he who does not ask a question remains a fool forever.

Chinese Proverb

You need to ask questions to understand your customer's needs and wants. Sounds simple, doesn't it? It should be. However, most salespeople fail to do this. Why?

Instead of asking questions, the typical salesperson is trained to never ask questions—that way he can avoid a situation where he may get an answer (God forbid!) he does not like. Instead of asking questions, the salesperson drones on and on about the technical specifications of his product or how wonderful his company is and why any customer who doesn't do business with *his* company would have to be an idiot!

The "never ask questions" approach may avoid the stress of getting an answer that you don't anticipate, but it does not result in high sales. Low sales are a lot more stressful than dealing with the answers to your questions.

The Millionaire Selling Secret of asking questions is the *proactive* approach to learning the needs of your customer and how to meet those needs. If you don't ask questions, you are just like the child who is blindfolded at the birthday party, swinging at the piñata. You know what you want, but you are blind as to what direction to go. So you swing wildly and hope that you connect.

I have a better approach. Let's take off the blindfold and start asking questions. So what should you ask? It depends on the product or service that you offer. With every product or service, there are certain universal wants and needs that go with it. Let's take a flat-screen television, for example. If you sell flat-screen televisions and you begin your presentation with the customer, you will want to ask questions that help you and the customer figure out exactly what kind of flat-screen television is right for the customer. You may ask the customer about where he plans to use it. In the living room, den, office, basement, bedroom? How many people need to be able to see it? If it is for the bedroom, the customer may have a different set of wants and needs as compared with a flat-screen for the den to watch weekend football games with friends.

The key here is this: *you* start asking the questions; don't wait for the customer to figure out what he should ask you. After all, who is the expert here? Since you are the expert, you should prepare a series of general questions that lead to more specific questions about the wants and needs of your customer. And here is another secret—if you ask questions, make sure to *listen* to what the customer says in response.

A good technique to make sure that you really understand the customer's answers is to restate his answers in your follow-up questions to get clarification. In our flat-screen television example, you might say, "So, if I understand you correctly, you are looking for the biggest flat-screen that you can afford to use in your den, and you want it to be as clear as possible, so that you can watch Patriots football games with your buddies on the weekends." Then wait for the customer to confirm your understanding. When you summarize what your customer is telling you, make sure to paint a specific picture drawn from his answers so he can visualize *using your product*. In this case, your customer should imagine his den, see and hear the game, smell the pizza, and almost taste the beer!

This is a critical point—you must build your presentation around the unique aspects of your customer's life, so that he can *imagine* already using your product or service. Your customer will appreciate that you are listening carefully and understand his specific needs. This approach will increase your sales dramatically!

You must write down all of the typical questions that you will ask your customers. Then practice them until you can recall them automatically. Don't memorize a script—your customer will see right through that. You want to be confident, flexible, and prepared—and having the right questions to ask will help your confidence immensely, which will also translate into higher sales.

Don't build assumptions into your questions regarding specific benefits. For example, if you are selling flat-screen televisions, don't say, "You want the biggest screen that you can get, right?" Why would you assume that? Your customer might say, "No, in fact I have little room in my apartment, so it is going to have to be very small." Ouch! Keep your questions open-ended— never make assumptions about the customer's wants, needs, tastes, desires, and budget. If you ask good questions and listen carefully, you will get your answers soon enough!

But don't get me wrong—you must have *one* critical assumption that runs as a common thread throughout your entire presentation, and that is the assumption that your customer wants to fix some kind of problem today and that you are going to help him solve his problem *today*!

ACTION STEPS

1. Make a list of all of the questions that you want to ask your customer, to discover his needs and wants. Start with general questions, and depending on his answers, move on to more specific questions as you get more details. Your general questions should seek answers to who, what, when, where, and why.

2. Make a list of all of the typical answers that you may get to your questions. This will build your confidence in dealing with answers.

3. Practice summarizing your customer's answers when you ask for clarification.

4. Go to www.brettbacon.com for additional tools and information on how to ask effective questions.

CHAPTER 15
BUILD YOUR ROAD MAP TO THE BEST VALUE FOR YOUR CUSTOMER

If you don't know where you are going, any road will get you there.

Lewis Carroll

Your questions allow you to build an accurate road map to what the customer wants and needs out of your product or service. In this way, your offering will provide the best value for your customer because it is tailored to his particular needs.

Best value is not always about price. When I use the term best value, I mean all of the benefits combined, specifically tailored to your customer. The best value choice might cost the most—it just depends on the wants and needs of your customer and whether you have charted a clear road map. If you have, you will know it because closing the sale will be effortless!

By asking questions, you are discovering what the customer is looking for—and believe me your customer will appreciate it!

Another huge benefit to asking questions up front is that you often eliminate many potential objections that your customer might otherwise raise. For most salespeople, objections are feared and despised all at the same time.

In the next section, I will convince you that you should embrace and love objections—they are an essential part of the selling process and your success.

You are laying a strong foundation for a long-term relationship with the customer when you ask the right questions. This is a key benefit to this approach. How so? Because on top of understanding the customer's wants and needs, you are also getting to know the customer on a personal level.

Asking questions sets you apart from the sales herd. Your customers are experts on bad salesmanship—they have seen it all! And so have you! The typical salesperson offers you a canned presentation, does not ask questions (except for questions up front, like, "So, how much money do you want to spend?"), ignores your objections, and argues with you as you head for the door! Does this sound familiar?

The simple fact is that if you are just slightly better than the average salesperson, you will stand out in the eye of your customer!

ACTION STEPS

1. Organize your questions and answers to build your road map to the close of the sale: you need to know what to offer to the customer that specifically meets his needs.

2. Organize your questions to identify the very same benefits that are attractive to your customer.

3. When you offer your selection of products or services, you can restate the very benefits that your customer has told you are important—this builds rapport with your customer and makes the close of the sale automatic in most cases.

4. Go to www.brettbacon.com for additional tools and information on how to ask questions to build your road map to what the customer really wants.

CHAPTER 16
QUESTIONS LEAD YOU TO THE HEART OF THE MATTER FOR THE CUSTOMER: "WHAT'S IN IT FOR ME?"

You must look into people, as well as at them.

Lord Chesterfield

If you craft your questions to drive toward the key question in the mind of the customer, "What's in it for me?" you will not only get the feedback to know what your customer really wants, but you will give your customer the opportunity to tell you what he wants.

If your customer *tells you* what he wants, through a series of skillful questions, you now have a solid grasp that you can weave into your presentation. On the other hand, *if you tell the customer the same thing,* he may doubt it.

This brings us to another important point. How much are you talking during the entire presentation compared to your customer? Most salespeople dominate the conversation about 98 percent of the time. I want you to do the opposite. I want you to let your customer do most of the talking, but in a proactive way—through the use of questions. To start, try to speak 60 percent of the time and let the customer speak 40 percent of the time. If you are accustomed to talking all the time, this will be very difficult to do.

But if you can hold your tongue long enough to ask questions and then listen very carefully to what your customer says, you are well on your way to mastering this Millionaire Selling Secret. Your sales presentation will run more smoothly if you adapt it to what your customer says about what's in it for him.

Your presentation will be more targeted—you will no longer be wearing a blindfold when you swing at the piñata. As you reach the buying decision in your presentation, make sure to restate your customer's own preferences and how they specifically apply to the choices that you will offer. And yes, you will offer choices to your customer. Even though you *think* you know after asking many questions and listening very carefully what your customer wants, you must allow for the possibility that he may change his mind at the last minute.

So don't paint yourself into a corner. If you have three choices in the targeted zone of your customer's preferences, let your customer make the choice, not you. This is very important. If you have several price levels of products to offer to your customer in the category of interest, don't assume that you know what your customer is willing to pay, even if he told you during the presentation. When it gets down to the moment to make the decision, your customer will often spend more or less money than what he said just a few minutes ago. So listen to what your customer has to say, but give him a little wiggle room to choose one price level over another.

If your products or services lend themselves to offering a good, better, and best choice, that would be perfect. I have found over the years that offering three choices is best for your customer to make a buying decision *today*. Four is generally too many to make a decision today for most people; he may want to "think about it"—the most feared words in the salesperson's world. We all want choices, don't we? So why not offer choices to your customer, as well? And if you offer three choices, be an honest broker. What I mean is, if you are going to offer three choices, then *really* offer three choices. Don't make fun of two of the choices and then tell the customer that he should obviously choose one over the other two because he is smart. If that is how you present, then you are really only offering one choice.

And even if you have one product to sell, you can always offer three choices, in terms of color, delivery dates, options, etc. So give your customer choices, carefully based on what you have learned by asking questions, and keep your choices limited to three, so that you do not overwhelm the customer. Besides, if you have done your job as the expert on the product or service, you should be able to boil the choices down for the convenience of your customer.

ACTION STEPS

1. Always look behind the customer's answers to your questions to find out what he truly wants.

2. Be prepared to offer your customer specific, tailored choices. Limit the choices to three: good, better, or best. If this does not apply to your product or service, offer three choices based on other characteristics, such as color, delivery date, warranty options, etc.

3. Go to www.brettbacon.com for additional tools and information on how to get to the answer to the customer's ultimate question: "What's in it for me?"

SECRET SIX.
THE MILLIONAIRE SELLING
SECRET OF *EMBRACING AND*
LOVING OBJECTIONS

CHAPTER 17
CONQUER YOUR FEAR OF OBJECTIONS BY EMBRACING THEM. DON'T IGNORE; ACKNOWLEDGE!

Do what you fear and the death of fear is certain.

Ralph Waldo Emerson

I love objections. I really do. I didn't start out that way. Thirty years ago, when I started my selling career, I feared and loathed objections. At the time, it seemed that the customer didn't like what I had to sell if he raised objections—or worse yet, he didn't like me!

Nothing could be further from the truth. Objections are a natural, important part of the decision-making process for the customer. The only thing I fear in a customer today is if I do not get any objections at all. That is a sign of a customer who is not engaged and couldn't care less about my product or service—so much so that he can't even offer up at least one objection.

So what to do with objections? Classic sales training says that you should ignore objections, on the theory that maybe they will go away. Essentially, this school of thought suggests that the best way to deal with objections is to avoid them altogether. Unless your customer is extremely stupid, forgetful, or forgiving, this approach simply does not work most of the time. Worse yet, it is just plain discourteous. If someone makes a legitimate objection, it is your job as a professional to answer it.

Here is an important opportunity to look into the mind of the customer. If your customer is raising objections, it is usually because he is actually imagining owning your product and is anticipating what issues might come up when using the product. Your customer is visualizing using your product! That is a very good thing! So you should not view objections as barriers to closing the sale. Instead, you should view objections as essential signposts to guide you and the customer to your destination: the closing of the sale and a happy customer.

This is your opportunity to make lemonade out of lemons! There are certain basic steps that you must always follow to properly handle objections.

Step Number One: Acknowledge the objection. This is often one of the hardest things for a salesperson to do—listen for the objection, pause in your sales presentation, and acknowledge the objection. So how do you acknowledge the objection? One example would be, "That is a really good question!"

Step Number Two: Thank your customer for the objection! Yes, thank him! Tell him you are glad he raised that question. By the way, never use the word objection in front of the customer. We know as sales professionals that the term is objection, but never use this term with the customer. While we are at it, never use any of the sales jargon that you have learned in the business, such as close or sold or deal or prospect or sell. Keep these terms to yourself. Instead call the objection a question or point. You might say, "You raise a really good point! Thank you! That is exactly what we should talk about next!"

Step Number Three: Restate the objection. That's right: not only do I want you to acknowledge the objection, I want you to restate it in your own words. In response to this, our students often ask, "Isn't that just rubbing salt in the wound? It's bad enough that I had to hear the objection the first time from the customer, now you want me to restate it?" The short answer is yes! Repeat the objection in your own words.

Why? Because a few amazing things begin to happen when you restate the objection for your customer. First, your customer will be amazed that you are actually listening to what he has to say. That will immediately increase your professionalism and integrity in the eyes of the customer.

You want to make sure that you understand correctly what the objection is and that your customer agrees that you have got it right. After all, if your customer asked you a question about the battery life for your product, for example, and you thought he was asking a question about battery costs, then you could launch into a lengthy answer that the customer does not even care about. Plus, your customer will be annoyed that you did not listen carefully. During your battery cost answer, your customer may be planning his escape from you and your sales presentation!

The third benefit to restating the objection is the opportunity to frame the objection clearly and simply so that you can easily frame your answer clearly and simply.

The fourth benefit is time. Restating the objection gives you time to think of how to answer it. If you are really unsure how to answer, then ask the customer clarification questions, breaking down the objection into smaller chunks that you can more easily answer, one part at a time.

The fifth benefit is confidence. You are showing the customer that you have the confidence to handle any objection—so much so that you embrace the objection by restating it and making it your own.

Step Number Four: Find the universal concern in your customer's question and tell your customer that some of your other customers have raised the same universal concern. The key Millionaire Selling Secret here is to never embarrass your customer by telling him that his objection is not a good one. I cringe when I hear experienced salespeople say things like, "Oh, that doesn't matter!" or "That is not important!" or "You don't need to worry about that!" or "You are wrong!" Does this sound familiar to you? If it is your goal to embarrass, alienate, and lose customers and sales, then make sure to tell your customer that he is wrong for feeling the way he does.

On the other hand, if you want to make your customer feel comfortable discussing his concerns with you, you must follow the steps in this chapter, especially telling your customer that it is a good question or concern. After all, the customer is king, and if he is concerned about battery life, then you should be, too!

This step is so important—no customer wants to feel stupid or foolish. And yet I see it happen all the time. My best guess as to why this happens so much is a combination of bad sales training and the salesperson's lack of confidence. Some salespeople fall into the trap of thinking that they must show each and every customer that they know best what the customer should get—and to do that they should tell the customer he is wrong. Believe me, the last thing your customer wants is to be told by you that he is wrong.

After all, the customer is the one who is going to spend his money on your product or service, so give him the dignity that he deserves by treating him with respect. In my book, any question is a good question!

Step Number Five: Answer the objection! Don't beat around the bush. Answer the objection in a direct, simple, and clear way. Don't fill your answer with jargon and highly technical words. As discussed in previous chapters, this is no time to hide behind your specialized vocabulary. Remember, a confused mind cannot make a buying decision. So don't confuse your customer with words that are not understood by the average person.

Step Number Six: Tie the answer to the objection back into your presentation or close of the sale. Never leave an answer just hanging out there! For example, if you have answered the battery life question and you are finished with your demonstration and you are waiting for the customer to make a product choice from the three options, you might say something like this: "Your first choice has the longest battery life—and that is important, as you have pointed out. Your second choice is rechargeable, which is nice because you don't have to replace the batteries. And your third choice has batteries that can be swapped out very easily for the least amount of money. Which type would you prefer?"

You'll notice in this closing question sample that I am asking for him to choose among three options. The assumption is that he will choose one of the three, so wait for him to make the choice—don't keep talking! Just wait. If he does make a choice, then you are done with the sale. Don't go over the choices again! You may talk him out of it. Once the choice is made, tell him he made a great choice and launch immediately into completing the order and taking payment. If he does not make a choice and instead makes another objection, no problem. Go through the same six steps and then return to the close of the sale.

ACTION STEPS

1. Write down a running list of all of the objections that you get. Ask other salespeople for their objections, too.

2. Once you have your list, start to break the objections into categories, so that you can form common answers that will apply to all of the objections in that group. For example, you will have a grouping of

objections about price. Another group might be about warranties and repairs, another group about delivery time, etc.

3. Now write out your answers to the objections. How they look on paper and how they sound when you say them are two very different things. Your answers can't sound canned to the customer. So don't try to memorize all of your answers. Every customer makes objections a little differently. This is why it is so important to restate the objection—so that you can start to standardize the way in which you frame your answer.

4. Go to www.brettbacon.com for additional tools and information on how to handle objections.

CHAPTER 18
THEN LEARN TO LOVE OBJECTIONS

The mind is its own place and in itself can make a heaven of hell or a hell of heaven.

John Milton

Once you have mastered the art of embracing objections, you are ready to graduate to the next level: learning to love objections!

Why learn to love objections? What is the point behind that? Because learning how to embrace and answer objections is not enough. You must learn to really enjoy objections, look forward to them, seek them out. In other words, learn to love them.

I don't care what you sell—objections are a part of the process. So you might as well learn to love the essential parts of the job. Or find another job.

I find that the unhappy salesperson feels that way because he has been trained to find misery instead of pleasure in what he does. In other words, if you have been trained to avoid objections like the plague, then you are going to be disappointed on a daily basis, because your customer will make objections.

But it goes beyond that—if you accept the fact that objections are a normal and natural part of the sales process, and you follow the steps set out in the previous chapter to embrace them—you will enjoy the process more because you have control over it. And your customers will appreciate that you are not ignoring them, which is the typical response that they get from salespeople. You will have higher sales as a result. This leads to a higher income for you and happier customers. So what is not to love about that?

So what is the Millionaire Selling Secret of this chapter? Learn to love and embrace objections early in the sales presentation. And this is important: do not wait until the end of your presentation to take objections! You want to take the majority of objections at the beginning of the presentation, not the end. Otherwise, you are going to run into big problems when you are trying to close the sale.

The average salesperson gets lots of objections at the end of his presentation because he tries to ignore and avoid them throughout the presentation. Your approach will be different. By tackling the objections up front, you will not have to deal with them (or will only have to deal with very few) at the end of the presentation, so you can focus on presenting clear choices to the customer.

If you are getting the dreaded "I want to think about it" too much, your customers are trying to tell you something. You are probably not identifying what your customers want up front, and you may be trying to avoid or sidestep altogether their objections up front. As a result, your customers are voting their dissatisfaction with you with their feet by walking out the door to think about it.

To minimize the "I want to think about it" challenge, answer each objection thoroughly and remind your customer of the solutions to his objections when you reach the end of your presentation and ask for the sale.

ACTION STEPS

1. Deal with all objections at the beginning of your presentation, not at the end. Write down your plan for how to structure your presentation to address objections up front, not after you try to close the sale.

2. Use objections to adjust the course of your presentation to the areas of concern for your customer.

3. Go to www.brettbacon.com for additional tools and information on how to benefit from objections.

CHAPTER 19
TELL STORIES TO ANSWER OBJECTIONS

If one advances confidently in the direction of his dreams, and endeavors to live the life which he has imagined, he will meet with a success unexpected in common hours.

Henry David Thoreau

Everybody loves a good story. Your customers will relate better to you and your products if you can weave your presentation and answers to objections into a good story. Take your experiences with prior customers and share them with your new customers.

If your customer is nervous about making the buying decision, tell him about others who have been nervous, moved ahead in spite of their fears, and were ultimately happy with their decision.

If you are new to sales and you do not have any personal experience with customers to share, then tell stories about how your company solved their problems and how you can do the same for your customer.

Get testimonials from previous customers and tell them as stories to your new customers. Testimonials are a very powerful tool—customers find it comforting and reassuring when other customers are willing to recommend your products and services. But too many salespeople rely on testimonials just for advertising campaigns. You can do better than that.

Your Millionaire Selling Secret is to weave customer testimonial stories directly into your sales presentation and answers to objections.

Every good story should have a hero. In your stories, the hero should be you or your company or the product itself. In order to be a compelling story, it must be true, relevant to the customer's concerns, and entertaining. This is not the time to brag or boast. Keep your stories short—two to three minutes is more than enough time to tell a compelling story.

Here is an example. When I want to make the point to a patient that hearing better can help to keep you safe, I tell the true story of the man who I saved from getting stranded on the highway. One of our patients is a retired master mechanic who I fit with a pair of new, custom hearing aids at the end of the business day. About thirty minutes after he left our hearing center, I received an excited telephone call from the patient. He said, "I wanted to thank you for saving me from getting stranded on the highway." "How did I do that?" I asked. "When I got in my truck wearing my new hearing aids, I could hear so much better. When I got on the highway, I could hear the high pitch of my fan belt. As a master mechanic I recognized the sound immediately. My fan belt was worn and about to break! I pulled my truck off the highway and just made it to a gas station before the belt broke completely. It probably had been squealing for a week, but I couldn't hear it with my bad hearing—until I started wearing my new hearing aids! So thanks for saving me from getting stranded on the highway!"

Patients love this story because it is real, it is interesting, and it has an unexpected ending. It makes the point in a vivid way that hearing helps to keep you safe in the world—which is a huge benefit to wearing hearing aids.

ACTION STEPS

1. Take inventory of your customer testimonials and categorize them by type of benefits to the customer. For example, you want to have one testimonial for price, one for quality, one for exceptional service, etc.

2. Go over every step of your presentation, and weave in a testimonial story into each stage of your presentation.

3. Weave testimonial stories into your answers to objections.

4. Go to www.brettbacon.com for additional tools and information on how to use stories to be more persuasive.

CHAPTER 20
DEALING WITH THE STRESS
OF OBJECTIONS

People are just about as happy as they make up their minds to be.

Abraham Lincoln

There is nothing either good or bad except that thinking makes it so.

William Shakespeare

Sometimes objections can be rough, especially if you can see that your customer is not satisfied with your answers. It can be stressful dealing with tough customers, their objections, and, ultimately, with feelings of rejection if a customer decides not to buy.

The Millionaire Selling Secret of dealing with the stress of objections, tough customers, and rejection is to accept the fact that sales is a numbers game—you must accept that you will not make every sale. But that is okay. For every no you get, you are one step closer to getting a yes from your next customer!

If you are expecting to get a sale 100 percent of the time, you are setting yourself up for a great deal of unnecessary stress. When you get a no, don't take it personally. Understand that you must accept some rejection to get to your next yes!

And don't dwell on your defeats. I have watched good salespeople get burned out by dwelling on a few isolated experiences with rude and harsh customers. Don't let this happen to you. Focus on your good customers. Remind yourself every day of the good that you are doing for your customers. Remind yourself every day of the financial benefits that you are getting as a result of helping your customers.

When you have had a rough day (and we all do), and everyone you meet that day seems to be against you, take the time to pull out your favorite written customer testimonials and review them. You need to constantly remind yourself of the good that you do and the good people you have met along the way. This is definitely a time to decide how you will assess your own overall sales performance—is the glass half full or half empty?

If you take the view that the glass is always half empty, you will always be disappointed by your results. It is easy to forget your victories if you only focus on your defeats.

On the other hand, if you think the glass is half full, then you are focusing on your victories. By focusing on your victories, you will recognize the progress that you have made so far that week, month, and year. Thinking this way is much less stressful.

You must learn to trust your own assessment of your abilities. Even if the world around you does not always see your potential, you must see it and believe it! Most of us are our own worst critics. We are quick to point out our own flaws and limitations to others. But this is the wrong focus—you need to focus on what your strengths are, not your weaknesses. Play to your strengths. If you are attractive, play to that strength in your presentations. If you have a compelling voice, use that, too. If you have an exceptional memory for details, use that. Whatever your strengths, make sure that you capitalize on them first and foremost. Then you can work on your weaknesses step-by-step.

Most of us were taught in grade school that we must have a balanced set of abilities. Remember what happened if you brought home a report card with an F or D, even if you had As or Bs in other subjects? What was the focus of your teachers? If your experience is typical, the focus was on your weaknesses, not your strengths. So we all learned at an early age to dwell on our limitations and not focus on our strengths.

The better approach is to focus on your strengths, your victories, your sales, and remind yourself throughout the day of your victories, no matter how small. This will help you deal with the temporary defeats and difficulties that you will encounter—no matter what. And learn to trust your inner coach—you know yourself best—so trust the inner voice that says, "Yes, I can do this!" If your inner voice is telling you right now, "No, I can't!" then you need to change the way you are talking to yourself! I talk about this in more detail in my book *Wake Up ... Live the Life You Love: In Service.*

ACTION STEPS

1. Keep a written list of your toughest objections, how you answered them, and what went wrong.

2. If your answers are not working, then you need to change them. Make sure that you understand the objection, you are restating it, you are answering in a simple and compelling way, and you are weaving in true stories of other customers who have triumphed over similar situations or concerns.

3. Read the book *Wake Up ... Live the Life You Love: In Service.* This book is a wonderful collection of essays by authors giving you positive, constructive advice on how to wake up and build the life that you love—in the service of others. Coauthors include Steven E, Lee Beard, Brian Tracy, Dr. Wayne W. Dyer, Dr. Michael Beckwith, and Ruben Gonzalez. Go to www.brettbacon.com to order your own copy, autographed by coauthor Brett Bacon.

4. Go to www.brettbacon.com for additional tools and information on how to deal with the stress of objections and the selling profession in general.

SECRET SEVEN.
THE MILLIONAIRE SELLING SECRET OF *PROVIDING THE BEST VALUE FOR YOUR CUSTOMER*

CHAPTER 21
CONCRETIZING THE
BENEFITS

All great masters are chiefly distinguished by the power of adding a second, a third, and perhaps a fourth step in a continuous line. Many men had taken the first step. With every additional step you enhance immensely the value of your first.

Ralph Waldo Emerson

I use the term *concretize* to describe how you must set the benefits that you offer in the concrete of your customer's particular needs and wants. And when I say the particular needs and wants, I mean the specific, unique needs and wants of your customer.

As you have discovered in previous chapters of this book, by asking questions, you learn a great deal about your customer—what is important to him and how he will specifically use your product or service in the story of his life.

Concretizing the benefits is another way of saying that you tell a story in which your customer is the main character of the story, and in that story your customer is using your product and service. And who are the heroes of your story? The customer, of course, as well as your product or service! The end of the story is predictable—your customer has triumphed by using your product or service to solve some problem that he had.

I also use *concretizing* to describe how you must present the best value of your product or service for another very important reason. Concrete is real, substantial, and when it sets, it is not going anywhere. If you have done your job right, your customer will also see your product or service cemented into his life.

Concrete is not abstract. I am amazed at how many salespeople talk in high-level abstractions about their products or services. By abstract, I mean a nonspecific, theoretical way to describe the benefits of your product or service. For example, if you sell life insurance, an abstract way of describing the benefit of peace of mind would be to say something like, "Many people find that this amount of life insurance gives real peace of mind." This is too abstract. It doesn't answer the customer's constant question, "What's in it for me?"

On the other hand, if you want to make it concrete, and you have done your homework, you will set the benefit of peace of mind in solid concrete by saying something like this: "John, this $1 million policy will give your wife, Kathy, real peace of mind because it will pay off your mortgage and leave her and your children, John Jr. and Anne, enough money to pay their monthly bills and live comfortably for years to come." I would then follow up with some more concrete examples by discussing how the death benefits of the policy will help to put John Jr. and Anne through college, etc. In this concrete example, who is the hero of the story? John, of course! And even in death, he is the hero because he made the smart decision to get enough life insurance to protect his family. So set every single benefit into the concrete of your customer's daily life. And if you are struggling to do this, it is because you have not asked enough questions to know your customer before you got to this stage of the presentation.

ACTION STEPS

1. Identify the benefits of your product or service and anchor them into the concrete of your customers' lives. You must use their names, describe the setting in vivid detail, make the customer the hero of the story, and describe in simple, concrete terms how your product or service will give them the tools necessary to be the hero of their life story!

2. Go to www.brettbacon.com for additional tools and information on how to concretize the best value benefits of your product or service with the customer's particular needs.

CHAPTER 22
COMPARISON TO THE COMPETITION

It is only by doing things others have not that one can advance.

George S. Patton

This is a tough one to do. The average salesperson does not want to talk about the competition for fear that the customer will want to investigate the competition first before making a buying decision. If you do not conquer this fear, your results will continue to be average.

The Millionaire Selling Secret here is simple: don't try to hide the obvious! It never works. If the elephant in the room is what your competition offers, then you better address it or you will only draw more attention to it.

Would you rather have your customer bring up the competition or would you rather have the control over when and how this elephant in the room is discussed? Obviously you are better off taking the lead on this. You can frame the discussion if you do.

Your willingness to talk about the competition is also a sign of confidence—a good quality to have as a salesperson and adviser to your customer.

So what should you say about the competition? The average salesperson avoids the subject altogether, and when the customer brings it up, he is quick to say something bad about the competition—usually with an air of

83

indignation. That approach is not for you. Remember, if you are not respectful of your competition, why should your customer be respectful of you? And you must never make your customer feel embarrassed or stupid for bringing up the competition!

You must find a professional way to distinguish yourself from the competition! The most important Millionaire Selling Secret to distinguishing your product or service from the competition is you! Your competition does not have you. You are your own unique selling proposition!

So make that your starting point. If you have developed your understanding of your customer's needs and wants, and you have won his heart, and you have demonstrated your professionalism and integrity, then you become a big part of the best value offering to your customer!

Once you set the foundation of your value to the customer, you can go on to distinguish some of the other specific, concrete ways in which your product or service is different from the competition. But don't make the mistake of guessing what might be of importance to your customer. Let's say that you know that your competition takes longer to deliver the product than you do—so you make a big deal about your shorter delivery time. However, if you do not know if this is important to your customer, you are not going to be persuasive, and you will be well on your way to losing the sale.

You should also keep in mind that you may be beating up on your future employer when you say bad things about the competition. Your goal is to build a solid foundation of satisfied customers that you can serve for a lifetime, no matter who you work for. So always be professional when talking about the competition.

Another common mistake average salespeople make is to not really know what the competition offers. You must know your own product or service inside and out, and the competition's. If you are really good, you know the competition better than they know themselves! This is a great opportunity to show your customer that you are a master of your product or service, and that he should follow your advice.

ACTION STEPS

1. Be prepared to discuss the competition first—before your customer brings it up. This gives you the opportunity to frame the discussion.

2. Contrast the competition by starting with yourself! You are unique, and your customer needs to know that. Remember, your customer is not just buying your product or service—he is buying you with it! So make this a major selling point when you compare and contrast the competition.

3. Know what your competition offers better than they do!

4. Practice describing the competition in fair and neutral terms. If you always talk down about the competition, you will look bad in the eyes of your customer. So take the high road and keep your discussion of the competition fair and balanced.

5. Never make your customer feel embarrassed about bringing up the competition. You should beat him to the punch, but if you do not, don't start slinging mud at the competition—you will probably get some on yourself in the process!

6. Go to www.brettbacon.com for additional tools and information about dealing with the competition in your presentations.

CHAPTER 23
GIVE MORE THAN THEY EXPECT

There is only one way to succeed in anything, and that is to give it everything.

Vince Lombardi

If you are just giving your customers the bare minimum required by the sale, you will only achieve average results. You must look for every way possible to give your customers more than they expect—from the moment you first meet to the moment you hand over the product at delivery.

Giving your customers more than they expect does not mean that you have to spend more money. Quite the contrary; usually the best extra benefits cost you nothing, like offering your customer a cup of coffee in the waiting room or calling him after delivery to make sure he is happy.

This is a great Millionaire Selling Secret: do more than your customer expects! You will set yourself apart from the other 99 percent of salespeople if you do. And this is easy to do. Why? Because the average sales experience is so bad! So it doesn't take much to stand out from the crowd.

I'll give you an example. I was in one of our retail hearing centers, and the last patient of the day was an elderly gentleman in his nineties. It was the middle of the winter in New England, and it was getting dark outside. At five o'clock, as we finished up the testing and sale, I noticed that it was snowing heavily outside and all of the cars in the parking lot were buried in snow.

The customer went out the door and slowly started scrapping the snow from his windshield. I didn't even think about it; I took off my lab coat and went out and cleaned off his car. He was a proud man—he did not ask for help—but I could tell that he really appreciated it. He thanked me, and I forgot all about it.

It turned out that this patient was a well-known town father in his small hometown. I didn't know that at the time, but I discovered it quickly because he referred so many new patients to our hearing center, and they all shared the story of the help I gave him during the snowstorm. I helped our patient because I wanted to help, not because I expected any sales benefit from it. But this is the funny thing about helping someone—word gets around.

So think of every way that you can go above and beyond the call of duty when you sell and serve your customers. Your kindness and professionalism will stand out in a world of mediocre customer service, and you will be rewarded with loyal customers and incredible referrals!

Another way to impress your customers is to surprise them with a small gift. It does not have to be expensive, but it must be a little different from what they expect—no company pens or calendars. You want to be different. So think of something small and inexpensive that you can give to your prospects and customers that they would appreciate.

For example, in one of our companies, we give every single new customer a jar of specialty jam in a colorful paper bag. The jar costs about two dollars. Our average sale is one thousand dollars. The customer appreciates the gift, and it can't be eaten and forgotten in sixty seconds (like a chocolate chip cookie, for instance). Everybody likes jelly and jam. Our customers take it home and put it on their kitchen tables, and every time they see the jar of jelly, they think of us.

I can't tell you how many times prospects come back to us and tell us that one of the key reasons they came back was the gift jar of jelly! They are impressed by our kind and unusual gesture, and they want to buy from a company that cares about their customers. You have to figure out a way to really impress your prospects and customers. Once you figure out what you want to do, you must do it consistently for it to be of value.

ACTION STEPS

1. Identify several free things that you can do to really impress your prospects and customers.

2. What can you give away as a gift to your prospects and customers? It must have a high perceived value, be out of the ordinary, and be memorable. It should be something that they will not quickly consume or throw away.

3. Go to www.brettbacon.com for additional tools and information about how to impress your prospects and customers.

CHAPTER 24
GIVE THE LOGICAL REASONS

An investment in knowledge pays the best interest.

Benjamin Franklin

You should win the heart of your customer first, if at all possible, as discussed in previous chapters. Once you have won your customer over emotionally, you want to win his trust. Trust is critical to building a long-term relationship with your customer.

Once you have won your customer's heart and trust, you will need to win his mind by giving him the rational reasons to buy.

The average salesperson relies too much on logic to be persuasive. He uses too many facts and figures. Facts and figures are fine, but most people make buying decisions emotionally first and then justify the buying decision to themselves and others through logic.

The average salesperson also buries the customer in technical terms, jargon, and statistics. The customer is often overwhelmed and confused. Remember, a confused mind cannot make a buying decision.

The Millionaire Selling Secret to presenting the logical reasons to buy is to strictly focus on the facts and figures that are of interest to your customer. This is not about you. If you sell speed boats, for example, and you love the facts and figures about engine performance, you will be very tempted to tell every customer you meet about the engine. But you are going to fight that urge. If you have followed the steps to learn what your customer really wants, you will avoid this trap. You must be passionate about the things that your customer is passionate about.

Continuing with our speed boat example, maybe the biggest concern the customer has is how easy it is to load and unload the boat off of the boat trailer. So if this is the case, you will offer the facts and figures to show how easy it is to do this, and you will present these facts in the concrete of the customer's life, as discussed in previous chapters.

A very common misconception about sales in general, as evidenced by the vast majority of salespeople who do it, is to bury your customer in facts and figures from the moment the presentation begins to the moment it stops, with the customer either buying or running for the hills to escape the avalanche of facts and figures!

Now that you know better, you are going to stop burying your customer in facts and figures and follow the steps outlined in the previous chapters to determine exactly what your customer wants to hear for logical reasons to buy.

The secret here is to present just enough information to help your customer make the buying decision. No more and no less! So how much information is enough? It depends. If you are presenting a computer to an electrical engineer, odds are you will be talking a lot about the technology. On the other hand, if you are presenting a computer to the average person, he does not want to know about all of the technical features of the computer. He really wants to know the benefits—in plain English!

A recent study was conducted of American who buy high-end luxury cars (one hundred and fifty thousand dollars and up). The customers were asked a series of questions about what they wanted most out of a luxury car. The car executives predicted that engine performance would be ranked high, along with the unique design of the car.

Surprisingly, American customers overwhelmingly wanted three key things over all else in their luxury vehicles: a comfortable seat, a convenient coffee cup holder, and an easy-to-use hands-free cell phone connection to their cell phone. That's it. Not terribly technical, is it?

The lesson learned here is not to assume that the more your product costs or the more advanced the technology is, the more you have to bury your customer in facts and technology. Instead, like a detective, you must first discover what the customer really wants and needs. Then you can give the specific facts to the customer that logically justifies his wants and needs.

If you find yourself in the middle of a presentation and you are talking about the facts and figures of the product or service, look for these telltale signs of disinterest of the customer. 1.) The customer is not saying anything in response. 2.) The customer is responding, but not about the facts and figures that you are presenting. 3.) The customer tells you he doesn't care about the information that you are presenting.

Does number 3 above seem unlikely? Don't bet on it. I can't tell you how many times I have told a salesperson that I did not care about certain features and the facts and figures behind them, and amazingly, the salesperson ignored what I said and just kept on going with the same presentation! You can probably guess what happened next. No sale!

When it comes to presenting facts and figures, you want to use the "inch deep and a mile wide" approach. In other words, keep the facts and figures to a minimum to explain the benefits of interest to the particular customer in front of you. If your customer wants more information, then you will go two inches deep and a mile wide. If he still wants more, then give him more. But let the customer take the lead on how much information he needs to make a buying decision today.

One of the major causes of lost sales is burying your customer with too much information. Remember, a confused mind cannot make a buying decision. If you are getting too many "I want to think about it" objections, it may very well be that you are presenting way too much information to the customer to digest and you are forcing him to not make a buying decision today.

Action Steps

1. Make a list of the key facts and figures behind the major benefits of your product or service. Strip out of your presentation any words or terms that the average person would not know. Remember, you do not want to talk over the head of your customer!

2. Follow the steps outlined in the previous chapters to discover the needs of your customer and then present just enough facts and figures to support the buying decision.

3. Go to www.brettbacon.com for additional tools and information on how to present the facts and figures to support the logical reasons to buy today.

SECRET EIGHT.
THE MILLIONAIRE SELLING
SECRET OF *AGREEING WITH YOUR CUSTOMERS*

CHAPTER 25
THAT'S RIGHT!

Right or wrong, the customer is always right.

Marshall Field

A soft answer turneth away wrath.

Proverbs XV.1

When I teach clients to sell effectively, I teach them to never disagree with the customer. Let me repeat that—*never disagree with the customer!* Never!

Some experienced salespeople argue in response to this, "But my customers often say things that are wrong. It is my job to straighten them out. They will appreciate it!" Wrong! Your customer will not appreciate it! Your customer will feel embarrassed, angry, or just plain irritated by your disagreement.

One of my standard responses to a customer's questions or comments is to say, "That's right!" I say it so much that my students begin to say it, too. Let me give you an example.

Let's say that you are selling cell phones. And let's say that your customer says to you, "I will not be able to use this phone. The buttons are too small!" Now you may be tempted to argue with the customer to prove to him that he can in fact use the buttons. But this is not the Millionaire Selling Secret approach. You want to agree with the customer. So instead, say something like this: "That's right, many of our customers feel that way when they see this phone. I can certainly understand why you might feel that way. Can I share something with you? You would be surprised how many people felt the same way you do and then discovered that they could use the phone once they had a little practice. Let's try practicing by calling a few phone numbers to see what happens. What is your wife's cell phone number? Can we call her? Great!" (Now place the phone in the customer's hand and guide him through the process.)

It takes creativity to find common ground with a customer, especially when he says something that is seemingly wrong about your product or service. But you are not paid to debate with your customers and prove them wrong. And if you debate with your customers too often, the pay will be poor!

Remember, if your customer makes a point, he has a reason for doing it—and feelings to go with it that you may not completely understand. So don't hurt your customer's feelings. Don't embarrass your customer. Don't make him feel stupid. Show your customer that you are listening to him; acknowledge what he said, agree that it is a legitimate concern or point, and then answer the concern in a way that is not argumentative or condescending. That's right!

ACTION STEPS

1. Make a list of the common misconceptions about your product or service.

2. For each common misconception, write out an answer that acknowledges why the customer might feel that way, explains how other customers often feel the same way, and answers the misconception in a way that isn't argumentative or embarrassing to your customer.

3. Go to www.brettbacon.com for additional tools and information on how to agree with your customers.

CHAPTER 26
THE POWER OF REPETITION

Repetition is the mother of all learning.

Saint Thomas Aquinas

Repetition is truly the mother of all learning and skill. As a salesperson, you are the teacher. If you talk over the head of your customer, you will lose the sale. And if you fail to repeat the main points that meet the needs of your customer, then you have failed to cement your product or service to your customer's unique lifestyle.

The average salesperson fails to weave the repetition of the main benefits into his sales presentation. The point here is quality, not quantity. In other words, instead of burying your customer in facts and figures, you are going to carefully emphasize through repetition the main points that are of interest to the customer. In this way, you are teaching the customer the benefits of your product or service.

So how much is enough, and what is too much when it comes to repeating the main benefits in your presentation? It depends on your particular customer. For some customers, you will find after repeating the key points once or twice that your customer understands and you can move on to the buying decision. On the other hand, if your customer does not appear to understand, then you will need to circle back to the previous key points and cover them again.

There is no standard formula for this. You have to watch and listen to your customer very carefully to determine if he understands the key points. If he understands, then there is no need to cover the same ground again. But if he doesn't understand, then you should repeat the key points, but don't make it obvious. Use a different example to illustrate the same point—make sure it is an example of something from the life of your customer. Tell a story in which the customer is the hero and your product or service is the solution to your customer's problem.

You also want to take areas of agreement (and you should have plenty of these since you always agree with your customer) and repeat them by weaving them into the repetition of the main selling points. You want to remind the customer that he had a concern and that you answered his concern effectively. This is the time to build your case for the customer to make a buying decision today.

ACTION STEPS

1. Identify the main benefits of your product or service.

2. Think of several ways to illustrate each main benefit.

3. Go to www.brettbacon.com for additional tools and information about how to use repetition to make your presentations more effective.

SECRET NINE.
THE MILLIONAIRE SELLING
SECRET OF *ADVISING YOUR*
CUSTOMER

CHAPTER 27
YOU ARE SELLING YOUR
ADVICE TO THE CUSTOMER

If there is any one secret of success, it lies in the ability to get the other person's point of view and see things from that person's angle as well as from your own.

Henry Ford

You are selling your advice to your customer, no matter what you sell. If you are passionate about what you sell, you understand your customer's wants and needs, and your customer trusts you, then you have set the foundation to properly advise your customer.

You may be thinking, "What if I sell a product? Am I really selling my advice?" The answer is most definitely yes! After all, what are you advising your customer to do? You are advising your customer to buy the product that meets his needs.

In most sales transactions, the customer may be overwhelmed by the technology, choices, options, and features of the product or service. The customer is looking for a safe harbor to make a decision. That safe harbor is you. You are going to advise your customer to make the right choice. And the right choice will depend first on your knowledge of the product or service, and second on your knowledge of the customer's unique wants and needs.

You must see yourself as a professional adviser to your customer—like a lawyer or a broker or an accountant. You always put the interests of your customer first. Don't even think about how the sale might benefit you during the presentation. There will be plenty of time for that after the sale. You need to focus exclusively on what is best for your customer.

If you think of your job in this way, as a professional adviser, you will never go wrong in your advice to the customer. And your customer will respect and trust you even more when he sees that you are really advising him on how to make the best decision. Once your customer respects and trusts your advice, the rest of the sale is very easy.

Advising your customer is smart selling. Pushing your customer to make a decision that is only good for you, without knowing what is good for your customer, is hard selling.

Start using the language of an adviser in your presentations. Use phrases like "I suggest" and "I advise" and "I recommend." Make sure to tie your recommendation to the concrete details of the customer's life. An example of this would be: "Since you are traveling by plane at least once a week, this laptop would be the best choice in terms of weight and portability, which I know is very important to you. I advise you to pick this model or these other two choices in the same category."

The Millionaire Selling Secret advantage of being an adviser to your customer is that it separates you from the product or service. In other words, if your customer decides not to go ahead with a particular choice or recommendation, that is okay because the customer still sees you as his adviser, and he will take your recommendations on other choices that you have to offer. And if the customer accepts the product or service, it is big approval stamp on your recommendation!

On the other hand, if your customer does not see you as his trusted adviser, then he may link his rejection of particular product or service to a rejection of you. This is not where you want to be. You want all of your customers to value you and your advice first, and the product or service second.

Let's think about your long-term sales career for a moment. If you develop strong, trusting relationships with your customers who value your advice, then they will follow you to your next company, idea, product, or service throughout your career.

So start advising your customers! Your customers will appreciate it, you will improve your sales immediately, and you will set the foundation of your long-term career in the concrete of your customer relationships. Your customers will follow you throughout your career—no matter what you sell in the future!

ACTION STEPS

1. Look at your sales presentation from the point of view of your customer. If you were the customer, how would you expect a trusted, professional adviser to look, act, and speak? Do you look, act, and speak like a trusted adviser? Or are you just pushing products at your customers? Make a list of the things that you can improve: your appearance, the words you use, and the benefits that you can advise each and every customer about.

2. As a trusted adviser, you can't candy-coat everything that you say to your customer. If there is a limitation to your product or service, it is better for you to advise your customer about it. Your customer does not expect your product or service to be perfect—but he expects you to be honest about it. So make lemonade out of lemons! If there is a possible limitation to your product or service, get creative and figure out the advantages to the limitation! Maybe the limitation results in savings on the price or it makes it easier for the customer to use. It is your job as a trusted adviser to figure out all of the advantages and potential disadvantages of your product or service. You must be prepared to give your customer alternatives to the limitation, whether that alternative is another product or service or an explanation of how the limitation can be leveraged into an actual advantage to the customer.

3. Go to www.brettbacon.com for additional tools and information about how to build your status as a trusted adviser.

CHAPTER 28
THE PERSUASIVE POWER OF SIMPLICITY

Make everything as simple as possible, but not simpler.

Albert Einstein

Simplicity is a great secret in sales today! It is a secret because most average salespeople who I have observed makes their presentation way too complicated. There is a common misconception in sales that you must bury your customer in data, technology, and choices so that they will be impressed and amazed about the complexity of your product or service.

Most people do not want to know how the watch is made, yet we all encounter salespeople every day eager to tell us how the watch is made instead of discovering our needs and wants and offering a simple, straightforward solution to our problems.

I think that the basic reason that most salespeople overcomplicate their presentations is because they have not taken the time to know what their customer really wants. And since they do not know what the customer really wants, they throw everything, but the kitchen sink, at the customer, hoping that the customer will choose something out of the mess of choices that he is willing to buy.

This approach does not work well and is way too much work. I'll give you an example of this approach. One of our companies was recently in the market for a high-grade office copier. I met the salesman, and before I could tell him what I needed the copier for, he started to bury me in specifications, techno-jargon that only a copier salesperson could possibly know, and a two-inch-thick stack of copier specification sheets! He asked me to go through the catalogs and tell him what I wanted. I told him politely that if I knew exactly what model would fit my needs, I wouldn't need him. He still didn't get it! So I placed an order with another company.

Simple for our purposes means making the choices simple for the customer, so that he can make a buying decision today.

Remember, a confused mind will not make a buying decision today. So make your presentation simple and straightforward for the customer. Your job is to present solutions to the customer based on his wants and needs, and if you have established sufficient rapport, you will know what he wants, which usually comes down to a few choices.

So you must boil down all of the facts, figures, technology, options, features, and choices into a few simple choices for your customer. Don't make your presentation any more complicated than it needs to be.

The second part of the secret of simplicity is that your customers want you to keep it simple. They want to make a decision based on the boiled-down analysis that you provide as their trusted adviser.

So keep it simple! And don't worry about not giving your customer enough information. If you have followed the previous steps in this book, he will feel comfortable enough to ask for more information if he wants it!

We all lead busy lives. There do not seem to be enough hours in the day! So don't add to your customer's busy life by dumping more work on him! As Henry David Thoreau said, "Simplify, simplify, simplify!"

ACTION STEPS

1. Boil down all of the features and technology in your product or service into simple choices. As Albert Einstein said, you are solving a problem—in this case for the customer—so keep it simple. Give the customer the simple answers that he is looking for to make a buying decision today.

2. After every sales presentation, look for ways that you can simplify and streamline the choices for customer and incorporate them into your next presentation.

3. Go to www.brettbacon.com for additional tools and information on how to simplify your presentation.

CHAPTER 29
THE PERSUASIVE POWER OF NOW

I have been impressed with the urgency of doing. Knowing is not enough; we must apply. Being willing is not enough; we must do.

Leonardo da Vinci

So we have established that you must simplify your presentation. You are a trusted adviser to your customer; you do not want to burden him with more headaches. The next step is to meet your customer's needs today. Now! Not later!

The Millionaire Selling Secret of the persuasive power of now is this: once you have persuaded your customer to own your product or service, he will want it yesterday!

This is another area where the typical salesperson drops the ball. The customer says yes and expects the product or service now, and the salesperson stumbles through an explanation of why he can't have it now. This is a formula for disaster. Countless sales are lost due to the failure to satisfy the customer's needs now.

We live in a highly competitive world. Believe me, if you do not figure out how to get your product or service to the customer now, your competition will!

There is nothing worse than persuading a customer to buy a product or service and then losing the sale to the competition because you can't deliver now!

The persuasive secret of now is so great it is often the final, decisive benefit that persuades the customer to go with one company over another. If your competition can deliver it today, and you will take two weeks to deliver, what is the customer going to do? Odds are the customer will go with your competition because the competition is willing to satisfy the customer's sense of urgency today.

If you have done your job right, your customer has a strong sense of urgency to own your product or service. So once the customer makes the decision to buy, you must be ready to deliver.

While it is true that some products and services cannot be delivered today because of shipping issues, customization, etc., you must find every way possible to deliver as soon as possible. And if you have mastered the secret of now, you will always get your product or service to your customer faster than your competition. If not, you need to reassess every step of the process to find the inefficiencies in the delivery process.

One final key point: don't kid yourself into thinking that the delivery of the product or service is not your job because you made the sale and you may not handle the actual delivery. Every aspect of the customer's experience with your product or service is your job, even if you are part of a large team. You are the face of the company, and believe me, if your company fails to meet your customer's expectations, your customer will blame you, not the guy in the delivery truck who showed up two weeks later than what you promised.

As a professional salesperson, you must accept total responsibility for your customer—from the sale to the delivery and beyond. Remember, you are in this for the long haul, and your customers must be able to rely on you to help them when necessary. If you take those calls and handle your customer complaints, you will build an army of loyal customers.

ACTION STEPS

1. If at all possible, always have the product or service ready and available to deliver the moment the sale occurs. If immediate delivery is not possible, figure every way conceivable to shorten the delivery time. If your competition is faster, you need to figure out why and see if

you can make the adjustments necessary in your company to make delivery at least as fast as the competition.

2. Go to www.brettbacon.com for additional tools and information on how to help your customers now!

CHAPTER 30
THE PERSUASIVE POWER OF EASY

All truths are easy to understand once they are discovered; the point is to discover them.

Galileo Galilei

Making it easy for the customer comes in many different forms. You must make it easy for the customer to hear your presentation. You must make it easy for him to make a decision today. You must make it easy for him to pay. You must make it easy for him to get delivery. You must make it easy for your customer to reach you or to get customer service.

Does this seem like common sense? Voltaire said, "Common sense is not so common." It seems to be common sense that you would like to make it easy for your customer to buy. The problem is, I find the opposite is true with many sales organizations.

For example, a restaurant that refuses to take a certain credit card is definitely not making it easy to buy. I understand the business reasons behind not using certain credit cards (the credit card fees are higher), but how is this the customer's problem? If you deny any customer the use of his credit card, you are not focusing completely on your customer's needs. True, he may find another credit card in his wallet or pay by cash, but that little sting of embarrassment and inconvenience may not soon be forgotten. You could lose customers, which will cost you a lot more than the extra 1 percent charge you were trying to avoid!

The question always boils down to this: are you trying to make the sales process easier for *you* or easier for the *customer*? If you are focusing on what is easier for you and your company, then you are on the well-worn path of mediocre sales results. On the other hand, if you are focused like a laser on what is good for your customer, what would make it easier for your customer to buy, then you are on the less-traveled path of champion-level sales!

ACTION STEPS

1. Look at every step of your sales process—from presentation to delivery to service—and find every way possible to make it easier for the customer to buy today.

2. Go to www.brettbacon.com for additional tools and information on how to make it easy for your customer to buy from you!

SECRET TEN.
THE MILLIONAIRE SELLING
SECRET OF *ROLE-PLAYING*

CHAPTER 31
PRACTICE MAKES PERFECT

It's what you learn after you know it all that counts.

John Wooden

This Millionaire Selling Secret is one of the most powerful: the secret of role-playing your sales presentation. And it is definitely a secret, because average salespeople never role-play! And since they don't role-play, they never get the amount of practice needed to sharpen their skills *before* they get in front of the customer. They don't get the benefit of honest, constructive feedback from the other salespeople on their team.

You can read and understand all of the Millionaire Selling Secrets contained in this book, but if you do not practice them through role-playing so that they become an automatic reflex down to your nerve endings and the marrow of your bones, then you will never achieve the level of sales greatness that you are capable of.

Why? Because greatness comes from quality practice, and lots of it. You must develop what Malcolm Gladwell calls, in his book *Outliers*, "practical intelligence." You must make the transition from knowing these secrets in your head to knowing them in your bones. In the *Outliers*, Gladwell did a study of a wide variety of overachievers ranging from Bill Gates to the Beatles. All of these overachievers had one major factor of success in common: massive amounts of practice. The interesting lesson of the *Outliers* is that the most successful people are not always the most naturally gifted in terms of talent. But these overachievers all have practiced far more than their competition.

So if practice is so critical to success, why is it so rare in professional sales? There are several major reasons. First, role-playing with co-workers takes courage. Most people are afraid of performing in front of someone else. Second, it takes a thick skin to role-play. You must be open to getting criticism of your performance. Third, it takes effort to prepare for role-playing. Fourth, it takes discipline to keep role-playing on a weekly basis, especially long after you are told by everyone around you that you know it all.

But you are different. You are not going to avoid role-playing. How do I know this? The fact that you are reading this book puts you in about 1 percent of all salespeople. You are taking proactive steps to improve your selling ability! Learning new skills can often feel like a marathon; you start the run full of optimism and hope, but somewhere in the middle you start to wonder why you ever started the race—your legs hurt, you are tired, and you just want to stop. Role-playing comes into play just about the last mile of the race. If you quit one mile before the end of the race, then all of the effort that you put in up to that point will be lost.

So now that you understand these Millionaire Selling Secrets *in theory*, it is time to role-play and practice, practice, and practice some more, until they become effortless and instinctive *in application*.

Here is a critical point: when you role-play, you are always practicing the *fundamentals of persuasive selling*. The fundamentals of any game are what win the game, if executed flawlessly when it really counts. John Wooden, the famous college basketball coach, trained his players to achieve greatness on the basketball court by constantly practicing the fundamentals. Vince Lombardi, the legendary football coach, was fanatical about his team practicing the fundamentals.

You must do the same thing to achieve greatness in selling: practice the fundamentals covered in this book. Practice through role-playing with other sales people, your family, friends—whatever it takes.

You may be thinking that you get enough practice in front of customers. That is not practice. That is game time. *Practice is done before the game, not during the game.*

ACTION STEPS

1. Find a co-worker, a friend, or a family member to role-play with. Your partner will role-play the customer.

2. If you are role-playing with another salesperson from your company, you will take turns playing the customer.

3. Ask for honest, constructive feedback from your partner. Listen very carefully to your partner's comments and recommendations to improve your performance—and write down the key points in a notebook that you keep just for this purpose. Your notebook will be a great resource for you to refer back to and to check your progress.

4. If you can have someone else watch the role-play and grade your performance, that is even better.

5. Create a simple presentation evaluation sheet that everyone can use to grade your performance.

6. Go to www.brettbacon.com for additional tools and information on how to sharpen your selling skills through role-playing.

CHAPTER 32
BREAK DOWN YOUR ENTIRE PRESENTATION INTO STAGES

The quality of a person's life is in direct proportion to their commitment to excellence, regardless of their chosen field of endeavor.

Vince Lombardi

So you have found your partners to practice role-playing. You will take turns playing the customer and playing the salesperson. Ideally, you also have additional coaches watching the role-play. Your coaches will grade your performance as well.

The Millionaire Selling Secret to effective role-playing is to break your entire presentation into smaller parts. This is critical for several reasons. First, role-playing is all about repetition and focus. You can't focus on improving your entire presentation all at once—it is too much to get your arms around.

So let's break down your sales presentation into smaller chunks. Start with the greeting. Psychologists tell us that most people reach their first impression of someone they meet for the first time in the first sixty seconds. Psychologists also tell us that most people stick with their first impression, even if it is wrong! So your greeting is very important. You need to practice it.

Depending on your sales situation, you may meet your client in your retail center or showroom, in your office, in their office, etc. But you need a plan. You need to write down what you plan to say and do in the first sixty seconds that you meet your prospect for the first time. Then you need to role-play it with your partner.

Here are a few tips in this critical first part of your sales presentation: don't overdo it! Don't run over your prospect by approaching too fast, and don't show the biggest smile you can manage. When you first get within eyesight of your prospect, stand and pause for just a moment—about two seconds is fine. Actors know how important this is. The next time you watch a professional theater presentation, notice how the actor will pause for a moment once he is on stage. This momentary silence causes the audience to focus on the actor, so that the actor can have maximum impact on the audience. You can do this, too.

When you smile (and you must smile!), make it a warm, genuine smile that shows that you are glad to meet your prospect. Why not offer the biggest smile that you can? Because it will not feel genuine to the prospect. You will put him on guard. After all, most people don't do this unless they see family members or close friends. Reserve your best smile until you start to get to know your prospects and they get to know you. You can role-play your greeting with your partner, and if there are more salespeople available, that is even better.

Here is another Millionaire Selling Secret to effective role-playing: it is the repetition of role-playing on a regular basis that really counts. You can't role-play once and expect to develop the champion level of selling skills that you have within you. How often do I recommend that you role-play? Role-play once a week. Pick a day that is the most flexible and everyone is most receptive to. Friday mornings tend to be a good day for the employees of our companies, for example.

Once a week? Yes, you read it right. Is it overkill? Not if you want to be a top producer and achieve wealth through selling. Let's think about this for a moment. Let's compare this to sports. Imagine that you are playing against a baseball team that never practices before the game. But your team practices once a week without fail. Odds are that your team will be the winner, because you have practiced the fundamentals.

When I was in the U.S. Army, I volunteered to go through the Army Air Assault commando training program. My fellow lawyers thought I was crazy! While I was at Air Assault School, our black-hat instructors had a saying: "Train as you fight and you will fight as you train." This is the training philosophy of the entire U.S. Armed Forces Training Command—to prepare soldiers to be physically and psychologically ready to fight when the time comes.

This is what role-playing is all about—preparing you to handle any sales situation through realistic role-playing scenarios. You will sell the way you train, and you should be very encouraged to know that about 99 percent of your competition never trains at all.

You should break all of the parts of your unique sales process into all of its component parts, including the demonstrating your product, answering common objections, closing the sale, preparing the paperwork, etc. Once you have done this, then you can begin to role-play each part.

Remember, you are training in the fundamentals, so don't stop role-playing just because you are not covering anything new. For a free sample role-playing evaluation sheet, which you can tailor to your particular product or service, go to our Web site: www.brettbacon.com.

You can organize your role-playing practices any way that makes sense for your situation. But there is one rule that I want you to always follow: once the role-play session begins, you must stay in your role until the end. You cannot stop and break out of character for any reason! Wait until you are done and then ask your questions or make your comments.

You will find it hard at first to stay in your role to the end of the session. You may forget what you were going to say or mumble your words or say the wrong thing. It doesn't matter if you make mistakes. Remember, this is *practice*; you are not losing money by making mistakes in front of the customer! So relax and keep moving through your role-play, no matter what. The most important thing that you will develop from role-playing practice is a sense of flow and timing to your presentation. But you will never develop the natural flow if you keep stopping and starting during role-playing.

The same holds true for the person role-playing the customer. He must stay in his role until the end of the role-playing session.

ACTION STEPS

1. Break down your entire sales presentation, from the greeting to the good-bye, into smaller parts. Include a special role-playing session just for handling objections.

2. Get your role-playing partners to agree to meet once a week for thirty minutes to practice. Plan each role-playing topic at least one week in advance, so that everyone can prepare.

3. Write down what you learn in your role-playing notebook.

4. Make it fun. Bring donuts for the session, pizza, etc.

5. Don't let your co-workers who are unwilling to participate discourage you. Soon you will surpass your critics in sales numbers!

6. Go to www.brettbacon.com for additional tools and information on how to role-play effectively.

CONCLUSION

There is no passion to be found playing small—in settling for a life that is less than the one you are capable of living.

Nelson Mandela

You are capable of greatness in selling. Don't let anyone tell you otherwise. No one is born a great communicator or a natural salesperson. The skills of selling and communicating persuasively are learnable skills, no matter what your background or current occupation.

If you closely follow the Millionaire Selling Secrets presented in this book, you will improve. And if you role-play a great deal, you will improve even faster!

So let's review what you have learned about the ten Millionaire Selling Secrets.

1. Assuming Your Inevitable Success

   ✓ You are always selling yourself.

   ✓ Always assume the sale.

   ✓ Always assume you will become a millionaire.

2. Building Passion for What You Do

   ✓ You will find passion in the benefits that you provide to your customers.

✓ Show your passion—how you say it is more important than what you say.

✓ Repeat your sales mantra every day.

✓ Passion is contagious—if you are passionate about what you can do for your customer, your customer will be passionate about doing business with you.

3. Making a Meaningful Contribution to Your Customers

✓ Focus like a laser on how you can improve your customer's life, not yours.

✓ Prove to your customer that you can be trusted, and once you have his, trust never take it for granted.

4. Building Strong Relationships with Your Customers

✓ Long-term relationships are the key to your long-term success.

✓ Communicate with your customer in a speaking style that is comfortable for him.

✓ Ask for referrals from your customers, and they will be your ultimate source of future business.

5. Asking Questions to Build Your Road Map of Persuasion

✓ Asking questions is the key to unlocking your customer's needs and wants. There is no need for guesswork.

✓ Once you know what your customer wants, you can follow your road map to solving his problems.

✓ Asking questions and learning what your customer really wants is the best way to answer your customer's ultimate question: "What's in it for me?"

6. Embracing and Loving Objections

✓ Don't ignore objections; acknowledge them!

✓ Thank your customer for the objection!

✓ Restate the objection. This shows you are listening carefully, and you can clarify the objection. Restating the objection also allows you to get agreement from your customer that you understand the objection and gives you time to think of your answer. It shows your customer that you have confidence because you are not ducking the objection.

✓ Find the general concern in the objection that is similar to other customers' objections. Tell your customer that it is a good objection and that other customers have shared the same type of concern and went on to own your product or service. Never make your customer feel embarrassed by your response to the objection. All objections are good—your customer feels that it is important, so you should, too. Give your customers the respect that they deserve.

✓ Answer the objection! Use plain English. Don't speak in techno-babble or jargon that the average fifth-grader would not understand.

✓ Tie the answer to the objection back into your presentation or close of the sale.

✓ For each new objection, follow the same steps outlined above.

✓ Never postpone answering objections until the end of your presentation! You want to answer the key objections at the beginning of your presentation, not the end. This approach will make it much easier to close the sale.

✓ Answer objections with stories about other customers who have had positive experiences that have answered the objection.

✓ Use relevant customer testimonials to answer objections.

✓ Your stories of solving objections must always have a hero: you, your product, or your company.

✓ Eliminate the stress of objections by recognizing that all objections are buying signals, not a personal rejection of you.

✓ Eliminate the stress of objections by understanding that sales is a numbers game—you need to see a certain number of customers on average before you make a sale. Each time you get a no, you are one step closer to getting a yes!

✓ Eliminate the stress of objections by focusing on the customers who you have helped. Don't dwell on lost sales too much, or tough prospects who did not buy. Focus on your strengths and your victories.

7. Providing the Best Value for Your Customers

✓ Set in concrete the benefits of your product or service according to the particular needs and wants of your customer.

✓ You set the benefits of your product in concrete by telling a story in which your customer is the main character and the customer is using your product or service! Who is the hero of the story? Your product or service, of course!

✓ Talking in concrete terms means that you use the particular specifics of your customer's life in the story illustrating your product or service's benefits—use his name, family members, etc. Be descriptive. If your product cleans garage floors, then you better know what kind of garage your customer has and be able to describe it in some detail. Then feedback the detail in your story about the success of your product or service and how it will solve a real problem that you know your customer wants to solve!

✓ Know your competition better than they know themselves. Don't hide from the competition—you can bet that your customer is thinking about them! Show confidence and distinguish yourself from the competition. What do you have that the competition does not have? You of course! You need to make this point to your customer! Even if your product or service is identical to the competition (which I doubt), you can still emphasize the importance of you to the customer—as a trusted adviser, a resource, and someone he can always depend on for help and great service!

✓ Give your customers more than they expect! This Millionaire Selling Secret alone will guarantee your long-term success if you practice it every day. Your customers will be loyal to you and send you referrals for future sales!

✓ Once you have won the hearts and trust of your customers, give them the logical reasons for the sale. But don't bury them in facts and figures—focus on the information that is of particular interest to your particular customer. Don't standardize your facts and figures! Tailor your logical reasons for the sale to what you have learned about your particular customer.

8. Agreeing with Your Customers

   ✓ Never disagree with your customer! Never!

   ✓ Build repetition of your major selling points into your presentation. Most people need repetition to absorb the main points. If your customer does not understand a major point, then repeat again using a different example. You cannot be obvious about your repetition. Be patient—your presentation is obvious to you but your customer is hearing it for the first time, so be ready to creatively repeat the major points in different ways.

9. Advising Your Customers

   ✓ You are selling your advice to your customer, no matter what you sell!

   ✓ Even if it is a product, you are selling your advice that your customer should buy the product.

   ✓ As a trusted adviser, you must look and speak the part. Tie your recommendations to the concrete details of your customer's life.

10. Practicing by Role-Playing

    ✓ Role-play your sales presentation before you get in front of your customer!

    ✓ Keep role-playing with your co-workers, friends, and family on a weekly basis.

    ✓ Write down the tough objections and difficulties that you experience in front of customers, and practice in role-playing how to deal with them.

    ✓ Always practice the fundamentals of your presentation.

    ✓ Keep practicing even after you feel that you know it all.

✓ Break down your entire sales presentation, from the greeting to the completion of the order, into smaller chunks. Role-play the smaller chunks. One week you might practice the greeting, the next week the demonstration, the next week handling objections, etc.

Resources

Recommended Web sites

www.brettbacon.com

www.briantracy.com

www.doneforyouwriting.com

www.drwaynedyer.com

www.joevitale.com

www.tomhopkins.com

www.tonyrobbins.com

www.mylifefranchise.com

www.mylifehearing.com

www.rickfrishman.com

www.waitley.com

Recommended Books

Assaraf, John. *The Answer: Your Guide to Achieving Financial Freedom and Living an Extraordinary Life*. New York, New York: Simon & Schuster, 2009.

E, Steven; Beard, Lee; **Bacon, Brett**; Dyer, Wayne, Dr.; Tracy, Brian, Ruben Gonzalez, et al. *Wake Up ... Live the Life You Love: In Service*. Little Seed Publishing, 2009.

Dyer, Wayne. *The Power of Intentions*. Carlsbad, California: Hay House, Inc., 2005.

Frishman, Rick. *Author 101, Bestselling Book Proposals*. Avon, Massachusetts: Adams Media, 2005.

Gladwell, Malcolm. *Outliers: Story of Success*. New York, New York: Hachette Book Group, 2008.

Gonzalez, Ruben. *The Courage to Succeed*. Aspen Press, 2004.

Hopkins, Tom. *The Certifiable Salesperson*. Hoboken, New Jersey: John Wiley & Sons, Inc., 2004.

Robbins, Anthony. *Unlimited Power*. New York, New York: Simon & Schuster, 1986.

Scott, Sophfronia. *Doing Business By The Book*. Charleston, South Carolina: Advantage Media Group, 2008.

Sherman, Andrew: *Road Rules: Be the Truck. Not the Squirrel*. Charleston, SC: Advantage Media Group, 2009.

Tracy, Brian. *Reinvention: How to Make the Rest of Your Life the Best of Your Life*. New York, New York: AMACOM, 2009.

Vitale, Joe. *Hypnotic Writing*. Hoboken, New Jersey: John Wiley & Sons, Inc., 2007.

AFTERWORD

A man is but a product of his thoughts. What he thinks, he becomes.

Mahatma Gandhi

I wish you the very best in your sales career! Please let us know how the Millionaire Selling Secrets work for you! We welcome your success stories, thoughts, comments, and suggestions. Please send your e-mail to: feedback@ brettbacon.com. Thank you.

MyLife Hearing Aids Franchise

The Opportunity

There has never been a better time to enter the hearing aid retail business. It is estimated that today, 31 million Americans need hearing aids. And the United States population is graying in record numbers, which means an exponentially increasing demand for high-quality hearing aids over the next twenty years. Current statistics indicate millions of people continue to experience hearing loss in the United States. For example, in 2010, the estimate is 33.4 million people with a need for hearing aids! Twenty years later, the estimate explodes to 43.7 million!

What We Are About

MyLife Franchise Corporation has pioneered a new groundbreaking hearing aid retail business model where the patient is welcomed to a highly professional, modern hearing center with state-of-the-art equipment and highly trained hearing specialists. We have taken the best retail practices from other industries and applied them to the hearing health-care field to create our world-class marketing, sales, management, products, and procedures.

Who We Are Looking For

We are looking for the best and the brightest to own and operate MyLife Hearing Aids Centers. If you want to help people and you have business experience, then you have the background necessary to join our team.

Contact Us

MyLife Franchise Corporation
Phone: 603-431-1220
Fax: 603-431-1104
E-mail: info@mylifefranchise.com
Web site: www.mylifefranchise.com
Mailing Address: 101 Shattuck Way, Suite 4
                                   Newington, NH 03801

MILLIONAIRE™
SECRETS

Go to www.brettbacon.com

Your Millionaire Secrets Internet Portal to Achieving Better Results in Sales, Marketing, Branding, Success, and Entrepreneurship!

✓ FREE Millionaire Secrets Newsletter

✓ Books

✓ E-books

✓ CDs

✓ DVDs

✓ Teleseminars

Brett Bacon—*Speaker*

Brett Bacon

If you would like to have Brett Bacon speak for your company, group or organization, please call 603-431-1220 for more information, or e-mail us at info@brettbacon.com.

Imagine what it feels like to be a published author!

Take the first step now to make your dream a reality!

According to a recent survey, 80 percent of Americans dream of becoming a published author! But few ever do. Why? Because they don't take action!

So stop dreaming and take action now! We are looking for talented coauthors for our next non-fiction business book in the Millionaire Secrets series. First-time authors are welcome. Be a coauthor of a chapter. We will show you how!

Do you have your own business secrets that you would like to write about? Upcoming Millionaire Secrets book topics include marketing, entrepreneurship, public speaking, networking, sales management, and success.

If you want to realize your dream of becoming a published author, then go now to www.brettbacon.com and click on the "Authors Wanted" tab for more information or e-mail us at editor@brettbacon.com.

MILLIONAIRE SELLING SECRETS

BOOK ORDER FORM

Internet Orders: Go to www.brettbacon.com.

Fax Order: 603-431-1104

Telephone Orders: Call toll free 866-480-1220. Have your credit card ready.

E-mail Orders: order@brettbacon.com

Order by Mail: The Bacon Publishing Group, 101 Shattuck Way, Suite 4, Newington, NH 03801. Bank Certified Checks or Cashier's Checks Only. Call our office for precise amount: 866-480-1220.

Please send the following books, audiobooks, ebooks or special reports:

> *Millionaire Selling Secrets* Paperback Book, Price $14.95 Each, Canada $19.95 Each, Qty _____

> *Millionaire Selling Secrets* eBook, Price $12.95 Each, Qty _____

> *Wake Up ... Live the Life You Love: In Service,* Paperback Book, Price USA $14.95, Canada $19.95 Each,

Qty _____

Please send me free information:

__Other Books__Speaking/Seminars __Business Coaching _____ Millionaire Selling Secrets Certification Course

Please add my name to your Millionaire Secrets eNewsletter subscription (free for a limited time only) or go online to subscribe at www.brettbacon.com).

Your E-mail Address: _____

Name: _____

Address: _____

Brett Bacon

City: _____

State: _____Zip: _____

Telephone: _____

Sales tax: Please add 7.75% for products shipped to California addresses.

Shipping & Handling: UPS Ground $6.00 for first book or disk and $2.00 for each additional product (estimate).

International: $9.00 for first book or disc; $5.00 for each additional product (estimate).

Millionaire Secrets eNewsletter

Free Subscription Offer
(for a limited time only!)

You can subscribe to the Millionaire Secrets eNewsletter FREE by going to www.brettbacon.com.

Our Millionaire Secrets eNewsletter gives you valuable information and insights into a wide range of topics—ranging from individual and business wealth and success secrets to sales, marketing, entrepreneurship, networking and how to become a successful, published author.

Hurry—this free offer is only for a limited time!

Go to www.brettbacon.com to subscribe today!

BUSINESS/ECONOMICS

Become a Millionaire By Using These Proven Millionaire Selling Secrets!

"Brett Bacon reveals the secrets to sales success in *Millionaire Selling Secrets*. This is a timely book—you will learn how to sell smarter and get better results immediately." —Rick Frishman, founder, Planned TVArts, publisher, Morgan James Publishing
www.rickfrishman.com

Imagine what it would be like to become a self-made millionaire by using these simple, fast, and easy Millionaire Selling Secrets! Would you like to dramatically improve your selling skills? If you are not getting the sales that you want *right now* and you want to achieve the freedom, respect, and security of becoming a self-made millionaire by mastering these millionaire secrets of persuasion, then this book is for you!

In this book, you will discover *how to*:

- ✓ Harness the power of assumption to achieve your personal and financial goals.

- ✓ Discover passion in your work.

- ✓ Ask smart questions to achieve incredible sales success.

- ✓ Embrace objections and turn them into sales.

- ✓ Build instant rapport, trust, and credibility with your customers.

- ✓ Eliminate the stress of rejection in sales.

- ✓ Help your customers to enjoy a better life.

- ✓ Make more money faster with Millionaire Selling Secrets.

Brett Bacon is coauthor of *Wake Up ... Live the Life You Love: In Service. Copyright 2009.* Coauthors include Steven E, Lee Beard, Brian Tracy, Dr. Wayne W. Dyer, and Ruben Gonzalez. From the best-selling series.

Brett Bacon is founder, CEO, and president of the MyLife Franchise Corporation and has thirty years of selling experience. He has personally sold millions of dollars of products and services and has coached others to do the same thing. He is a successful entrepreneur, attorney, business coach, speaker, and author.

All self-made millionaires have one thing in common—they use the secrets of persuasion found in this book. Now you can discover their secrets for the first time! Would you like to sell your way to becoming a millionaire? Then get started today!

To learn about our other products and services, and to subscribe to our Millionaire Secrets eNewsletter *free* for a limited time, visit our Web site at: **www.brettbacon.com.**

INDEX